ENCOUNTERS WITH WALES

Encounters with Wales

T. Robin Chapman

GOMER

First Impression—October 1995

ISBN 1 85902 286 3

© T. Robin Chapman

All rights reserved. No part of this book may be reproduced, stored in a retrieval system, or transmitted in any form or by any means, electronic, electrostatic, magnetic tape, mechanical, photocopying, recording or otherwise without permission in writing from the publishers, Gomer Press, Llandysul, Dyfed.

Printed in Wales at
Gomer Press, Llandysul, Dyfed.

To Susan, with thanks

Introduction

My interest in Wales has always been primarily an interest in the people who live there. What I remember most from my first visit, a family holiday in South Pembrokeshire in 1971, is not the landscape or the wildlife I had ostensibly been brought to see, but a snatch of conversation at a supermarket check-out in Haverfordwest. 'When she come out of Withybush,' one woman was saying, 'you could have put your fingers like that round her arms.' She held up a curled index finger and thumb six inches or so from her face, closing one eye the better to focus, defying her neighbour to disbelieve her. 'Like that,' she insisted. 'Nothing on her.' It was the curious mixture of the mundane and the unfamiliar that attracted me, shared references to a place and a person I could only imagine.

A year later I began to learn Welsh. I was still young enough to make a fool of myself, stopping strangers on the street to ask them the time for practice, eavesdropping on virtually unintelligible conversations, coping with what appeared to me at the time to be insurmountable contradictions. I remember, for instance, my amazement at seeing Welsh speakers sporting Liverpool scarves at Bangor station on a Saturday morning. The dextrous, unselfconscious switching from Welsh to English in mid-sentence, English speakers living in houses called Bron Heulog and Welsh speakers calling their house Sunnyside: these things fascinated me.

This book has been an attempt to satisfy that continuing curiosity. My own position is semi-detached: fluent in Welsh but English by birth and living in Yorkshire. The interviews were collected randomly on a series of visits to Wales during the summer of 1994, in trains, in pubs, in people's houses, in offices, on street corners and – during one frantic afternoon – on the field at the National Eisteddfod. I employed only two criteria: that the people interviewed must live in Wales, and that I did not already know them. I simply asked people to talk about themselves and the Wales they knew. To this extent, then, the interviewees set their own agenda. I turned on the tape recorder, asked supplementaries when necessary and let them talk. The words on the page are more or less verbatim transcriptions of their words, with all their hesitations, false starts and trailing sentences. Some interviewees requested transcripts and these were duly sent. Welsh-speaking interviewees were given the choice of speaking in either language and in the case of interviews in Welsh (denoted by an asterisk) I have given as close an approximation as possible of the style of language used.

The best time to make approaches, I discovered, was between ten o'clock and half past four and again after eight in the evening. Even with that refinement the process was never easy. Approaching people cold on a street corner may work for vox pops requiring no more than two or three sentences, but anything more substantial needs both parties to be seated. I had hoped that if I sat for long enough in a public place looking winsome then conversation would develop automatically. No such luck. Interviewees had to be hunted down, introductions made, the background to the book explained and consent to record sought. At times it seemed that no one wanted to speak. I sat on a bench in Cardigan after several failed approaches and doubted the whole enterprise. Even after a good interview there was no guarantee that another could be found, but then a sudden opportunity would arise and people seemed almost to be queueing up. In Ystradgynlais, in Newtown, in Brecon, in Penygroes, again and again, interviewees presented themselves.

Most people were remarkably forthcoming, some even unguarded. I had very few refusals, but have used only two thirds, probably, of the total number of interviews recorded in the interests of balance. One English woman from Waunfawr, Gwynedd, said that she 'knew things about the Welsh and the way they go on that would make your hair curl', but, tantalisingly, refused to elucidate; an old man in Llanfairfechan said that all I wanted to know could already be found in the official history of the village; the operator of an Italian café in Merthyr who had been recommended to me as a good speaker said that he had already been 'done thousands of times. I've had the BBC here twice, HTV, the *Western Mail* three times . . .'; one man telephoned after a particularly good interview to inform me that he had perhaps said more about his employers than was good for his future career; one interviewee has used a pseudonym. Some places yielded no interviewees: Usk was wet and anyone with any sense was indoors; Llandrindod was full of hardy cyclists but seemed to have no native inhabitants at all; there was nowhere at all to park with impunity the whole length of the Rhondda; Cardigan was too busy with afternoon shoppers; in Dolgellau my tape recorder inexplicably refused to record a complete conversation; we reached Penrhyndeudraeth just as everyone else was leaving and Llanuwchllyn, despite being marked on the map, didn't appear to exist at all.

In compiling this book I visited places which had previously been no more than a sign on a by-pass or a stop on a railway journey. I have drunk tea in almost every county in Wales. In Llanbister, Powys, as the rain fell outside, Mr Harry Woosnam showed me photo albums of five generations of his family, Tegwyn Griffiths opened the Owain Glyndŵr museum in Machynlleth for me on a Sunday morning, and Mrs Davies the Postmistress at Carno gave me and an interviewee open house in the sitting room while she retreated to the kitchen. But Clwyd takes the prize for hospitality. Following a chance meeting in Prestatyn I was adopted as an honorary Piglet for the evening by the Hoggets, a group of drinking cronies consisting of a master butcher ('Boss Hog'), a retired schoolteacher, a retired publican, a café proprietor, a job centre manager and two policemen. After embarrassing myself partnering an experienced snooker player in Prestatyn itself (one red ball, one green, three whites) we travelled up the one in five hill to the Eagle and Child in Gwaenysgor in a mini cab from Roberts' taxis – the Hogmobile – where they drank bitter and I surreptitiously drank bitter shandy. A memorable and thoroughly enjoyable evening, marred only slightly by a remark from one of the Hoggets that if I wrote like I played snooker then this book would be lucky to end up as a one page essay. By nine-thirty the following morning interviews had already been arranged for me in Rhyl. My very special thanks to Mr Neville Hugh Jones and his wife for this and many other kindnesses.

I started with the mistaken idea that all conversations would be equally worthy of inclusion, but some interviewees, I suspect, told me what they thought I wanted to hear: a discourse on the dust from a retired miner in Treherbert and a paean of praise to 'our bardic tradition' from a Welsh student in Penmaenmawr. There seems little point in reproducing them here. There were lyrical moments, too. At the end of an otherwise unremarkable interview a man in Pontypool told me that his father had been a monumental mason and his mother a teacher of typing and shorthand. 'When she stopped, like, she sold off all the typewriters and I got one – the best one really. I've still got it at home – big thing, Remington – and I still use it, keep it oiled.' There was a pause as he made the connection. 'I suppose it's like a memorial to her, really, because my dad could never afford to make her a stone.' Women are slightly under-represented. With only one exception, when a couple was approached it was the man who did the talking.

In introducing a book in which so much is said by others on the state of Wales it is invidious perhaps to venture a comment of my own. But the picture is, I think, a hopeful one. I had half-anticipated that the book would be coloured by the stereotypical hostilities: mutual suspicions of North and South, Welsh- and English-speaking, urban and rural, natives, newcomers and visitors. This proved not to be the case. The Wales I encountered was self-assured and forward-looking. The fortunes of the language were inevitably mentioned, especially by Welsh speakers, but the attitude was always confident. Mrs Davies at Carno told me that children from the English Midlands who arrived with broad Brummie accents, *'yn twangio'*, as she put it, would correct her for not using Welsh with them within a few months and that their parents were delighted by their command of two languages. A painter and decorator, originally from Merthyr but now living in east Clwyd, had sent his children to Welsh-medium school for no other reason than 'that's the best thing for them, to know Welsh. No, I don't know much and not many round here speaks it, like, but it's a good thing.'

Of course Wales is changing – the European symbols on enterprise zones are evidence of that – but most people I spoke to saw change as an opportunity rather than a threat. Their great concern was for the next generation. Robert Roberts, a retired miner in Tredegar was typical. 'Give it another year or two,' he said of the town, 'and I think it'll do very well. I'd like to see a few more decent-sized factories coming for the youngsters to have a job. Whatever happens, boomtime or otherwise, it isn't going to affect me, workwise. But I'd like to see it for the youngsters all the same.' Even those who were dependent on a fluctuating holiday market were relatively sanguine about the future. Dylan Rowlands, owner of the Dylanwad Da restaurant in Dolgellau, spoke about the delayed impact of the town's bypass on trade from outside: 'Dolgellau seems to be dying on its feet rather . . . as far as the tourists go', but was pleased with the growing proportion of local customers, since he started up in 1988. David Roberts, a hotel manager in Anglesey, was leaving for a post in Newmarket on the very morning we spoke. Wales, he claimed, had missed the tourist boat: 'Take Caernarfon. There's no top-grade hotel there. How can you expect to attract visitors without?' Even he, though, praised Wales's natural advantages – 'fantastic potential' – and was keen to return when the opportunity arose.

How representative a sample I met is impossible to say – and inevitably to an extent it was self-selecting – but I came away from Wales impressed that total strangers could be so accommodating. There was no cynicism and very little suspicion. Only one interviewee, understandably so in a village plagued by tabloid journalists following a murder locally, asked me who I was and enquired into my background. Anthony Jones of the Carmarthenshire Hunt feared that I might be a saboteur, but did not pursue the matter. People said surprising, funny, sad and revealing things about themselves and Wales. The fascination is undiminished.

I am grateful to all those who consented to talk to me and to those who recommended others, as I am to friends in north and south Wales who gave me a bed for the night during my travels.

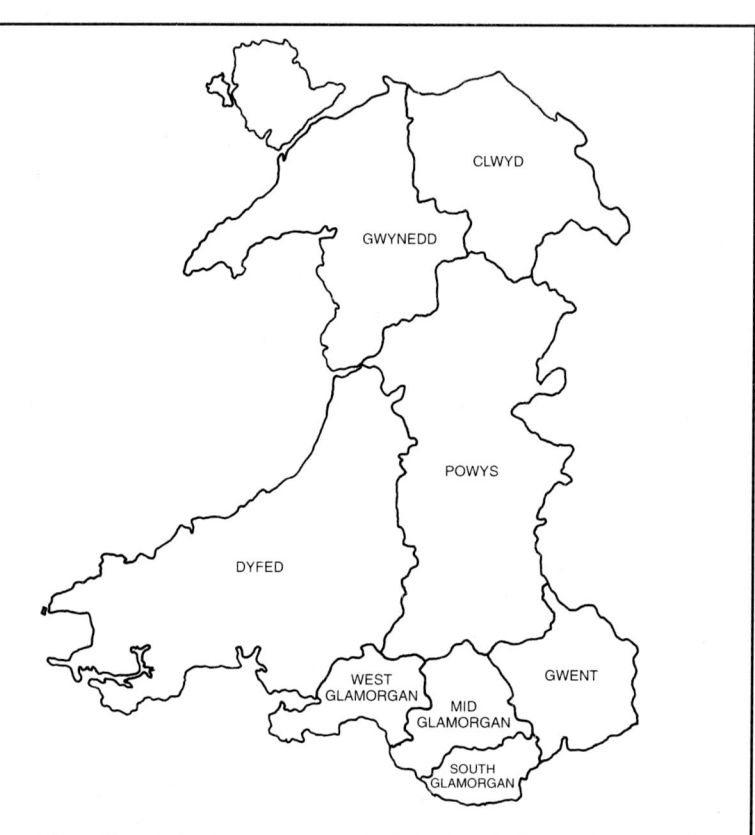

[Map of Wales showing counties: CLWYD, GWYNEDD, POWYS, DYFED, WEST GLAMORGAN, MID GLAMORGAN, SOUTH GLAMORGAN, GWENT]

When these interviews were conducted, the administrative map of Wales looked as it does here. By May 1996 the eight counties will have been replaced by twenty-two unitary authorities and my mental map of Wales will need to be re-drawn.

I am old enough to remember the outrage and confusion that greeted the demise of Radnorshire, Merioneth and the rest in 1974. 'I will *not* live in Dyfed,' someone from the St Clears declared in his local newspaper; 'it sounds like something out of Tolkien.' A friend from Wrexham spelled her native county as 'Clywd' until well into the nineteen-eighties. Now, rather like the new Methodist minister – never as good as the old one – reaching the end of his or her term, there is an affection for what is almost gone. A slogan painted on the wall of the Faenol Estate between Bangor and Caernarfon reads, *Cadernid Gwynedd yw ei Hiaith* – the Strength of Gwynedd is her Language. Will *Cadernid Sir Fôn a rhannau o Aberconwy a Cholwyn a Sir Gaernarfon a Meirionydd* inspire a future generation?

Kim Atkinson, Bardsey Island, Gwynedd

Kim was born in 1962 and brought up on the Island between the ages of one and six when her parents took on a farm tenancy there. She and her brother were educated at home by their mother. In 1969 the family moved to Cornwall, where Kim lived until going to art school in 1980. She did a foundation course at Falmouth, three years' painting at Cheltenham and an M.A. in Natural History illustration ('a perpetual student!') at the Royal College of Art. During her time at the Royal College she re-established her contact with Bardsey. She has lived there with her partner Gwydion, a native of Pen Llŷn, since 1987 and is a working artist.

Were you conscious that your upbringing was unusual? Were you a lonely child?

'I think it was important that there were two of us because we used to spend all our time mucking about, playing together. There were other children on the Island during the summer, but I don't really remember them because they weren't there long enough to form any great bonds, really. To us it just seemed normal because we were so young and couldn't remember any previous life. It was when we went to the mainland that . . . that seemed different at first. I quickly slotted into it because I was quite an outgoing child. But it was a very free sort of childhood. We used to be outside all the time and we had the run of the Island except for the steepest cliffs and the top of the mountains.

Do you look back on it as an idyllic time?

'I suppose it was, but we enjoyed childhood when we got back to the mainland as well. It wasn't that we were suddenly clamped down on; it was that we didn't have our own territory. You know, we knew the Island intimately and it was different when we got to the mainland because it was an infinite space. It wasn't an entity that we could get to know and explore.'

Does Bardsey seem as remote now, on second acquaintance?

'Well, we've got our own boat. That's made a big difference – psychologically – even if we don't go crossing the Sound every minute. But it is quite remote still, and you notice that when you have to get ashore for a deadline! I had to go over for an interview once which was cutting it fine. I left it until a week before, which in any normal circumstances would be ample time. For that interview, I actually got a lift with the lighthouse helicopter! That got me over there, but it's not something we rely on. That's the thing: you have to plan. When you're going anywhere you have to think about going about a fortnight or a week before you're due. It's just a case of forward-thinking, really. Basically, if the sea's rough you can't cross. I suppose as a kid I didn't feel it was isolated because we didn't have the responsibility of getting stores or getting mail or anything like that, but now it does seem frustratingly difficult to cross at times. But I'm prepared to put up with it! It's hard when I come ashore beacause I'm not used to driving in towns and things like that. I feel like an oik from the sticks!'

Are you conscious of having to readjust when you come back to the mainland?

'I don't know if I do readjust, really. It's almost easier to go straight to France where I'm all at sea again than conducting myself in Pwllheli, for example. I was over for a term because I did some teaching. I was an artist in residence at the Mostyn Gallery, Llandudno so that was into the deep end, dealing with children. For me, that was a really important growing-up thing, to teach and force myself to face that sort of work. Because it's all too easy – I feel myself doing it – to go back to the Island and just . . . it's safe there and it's a place I know and the people who are there I know usually and I don't have to join the human race too much. It's good to be challenged, I think.

'Last winter the population was down to four: a farming couple who have actually retired now and my partner and I. He works for the Trust that owns the Island – the Bardsey Island Trust. But the population's grown a bit since then and now there's an island warden and his wife and two kids and a couple who shepherd. But the thing is, in the summer it floods with people. So it's a very odd set-up really; there's a transient population. And another important thing is that it's not really Wales. It's like a little chunk of England. The only Welshman living there is Gwyd, so you don't hear Welsh spoken very often unless, say, the observatory boatman comes over. The couple who farmed are English and they were there for twenty-two years and were a fixture. In the days when my parents were there they were English and our neighbours were Welsh, so it used to be half and half. The Trust who bought the Island in '78 was set up by English people largely. I am conscious of living in Wales, though. Particularly because I haven't really learned Welsh. I mean, I do speak a bit and Gwydion is first-language Welsh. But everyday living, it could be anywhere because you don't hear Welsh spoken.

'Being on the Island is a very powerful experience in itself because it's a very small patch of land. I've often tried to evaluate what it is about being on that Island that's special because a few years ago we bought a cottage on the mainland at Uwchmynydd and we don't look at the Island from the cottage. It has a very different atmosphere. I think it's because there are so many more people around and it's a much more active farming set up. There are a lot more people you don't know. I suppose that's what it boils down to. Places you don't know beyond your immediate view. *Terra incognita*, really. Whereas on the Island it's your own little patch and . . . it isn't feeling secure, really; it's not in those terms. But it's a known landscape, a known environment. It is the only place I've ever lived in Wales so I can't compare how it would seem to live in Llŷn, for example. Gwydion was brought up on Pen Cilan and Botwnnog so he's very local and what's important for him is the community. You know, we go along the road and he's waving to everybody, he knows everybody. So for him it's like being on the Island because it's his own territory. He knows who lives on this farm, that farm. He's got much more of a network, structure, memory and knowledge built up over the years which tie him. Whereas for me it's the Island which is my known territory and memory. Something that we've noticed about the

Island is that people come here and they adore it straightaway and they say, "What a marvellous place, and how spiritual" – that's a word which crops up constantly. Spiritual. Really, they mean it as Christian pilgrims visiting because of the Christian heritage and they feel that spirituality. To me that's mysterious because I think my sense of that is childhood memory. But Gwydion, certainly, he doesn't feel it any more here than for example at Pen Cilan where he spent his formative years. That's where he feels to be home. So that sense of spirituality is something that people bring to the Island, in a way. It's something they're looking for, so they find it. If you live there it's not quite like that because you have to get on with the garden or go out and get a ewe in if she's having trouble lambing or get up a load of seaweed or go after driftwood or go ashore and buy a ton of coal. It just seems like everyday life crowds in.'

How do you work and exhibit?

'The work is no problem because I've got a studio and a mangle which I use because I do a lot of print-making, a mangle which I've converted to a printing press for relief prints. But getting the stuff to exhibitions can be problematic. I take stuff rolled and frame it on the mainland – or recently I've had it framed, which hurt a bit because it was very expensive. It was just a case of having to, really, because I ran too close to the deadline. But it's fine. It's a good place to be an artist because the visitors who come to the Island to stay, they're all happy to buy a picture. For me, that's great. But the main reason, I suppose, why I'm here still stems back to when I was a student, drawing birds. It's an important bird place: migratory birds stop there and there's a big population of breeding birds. Heaven, really, for anyone interested in drawing birds! I'm doing a print at the moment. It's a design for a card which the Trust wants to produce next year because there's a shop where they sell cards. The birds that I do are usually in a context: landscapes with birds. Recently I've become involved with a group called the Artists in Nature Foundation – it's a Dutch organisation – and they invite artists from all over the world: United States, Canada, Japan, China, Russia. They invite them to go off to places which are threatened in some way. And it's brilliant! We all go off and camp somewhere. The first trip was to Poland – the Biebrza Marshes in the north east of Poland – and we produced masses of work and it was all turned into a book. And on trips like that, my interest is birds; that fuels the work I do, but I also deal with the landscape, the interaction between farming, for instance, and birds – I try to branch out a bit. And this year I've been to Spain and the Loire Valley with the same group. It's good to get away from the Island and see different landscapes. It's quite inspiring.'

Do you anticipate living on the Island indefinitely?

'I don't know. It's that we really – both of us – live from day to day, year to year. We've talked about leaving because there are aspects to living on the Island that I'm not so happy with, which is the fact that in summer it turns itself into a holiday camp. Lots of people in and out. We get disturbed a lot because people are on holiday and they're happy to sit and chat. It can be almost too much of a good thing and it's an unnatural way of being. At times we've said, "Right, that's it. Let's go to the mainland." But we've got to think in terms of Gwyd's work as well and I don't think he'd just waltz into a job and it *is* a job and it's been made a full-time, all-the-year-round job for the last couple of years. So that keeps us here and of course we do like it.'

Nicoli Ann Bailey, Aberdaron, Gwynedd

Nicoli Bailey was born in Seattle, Washington in 1955, trained in cultural athropology with an emphasis on Californian archaeology and worked as an archaeologist for seven years. She then entered the legal profession, working initially in litigation and thereafter in mediation. Her 'passion' for Wales began in May 1993. She is currently taking a career break to pursue it.

'My interest began completely by chance because I read a book called *Here Be Dragons* by Sharon Kay Penman. I was off on a very short but very intense trip with my father to Hong Kong because he was retiring from the airline and wanted to take myself and my sister and his wife over there for his swansong and I needed some reading material because I was going to be in a plane for a long time and the book literally jumped off the shelf at me. I had no interest in Wales before then whatsoever. The book is an historical novel set in about the twelfth and thirteenth centuries here in north west Wales and I was riveted and completely enchanted by all the history here. She had two subsequent novels in the trilogy and I read those and that's what started me off on this . . . I don't even know how else to call it other than a sort of quest to learn more about Wales.'

What did you know about Wales at the time?

'You know, I don't believe I knew anything about Wales to be very honest with you. My connection with the British Isles was through several close friends that were English and I knew one Scots person from the Highlands and I really didn't have any concept of Wales whatsoever other than that several years prior to that, before my grandmother died, she had informed me out of the blue that her husband – my grandfather's father – had come over from Wales with his brother and I had always assumed it was England because of my last name. And when she said that it was Wales, she did plant a seed, I suppose, and I thought, Wales! God, that sounds much better than England to me! And that was it and I'd never done any research and I'd never been to the British Isles although I'd been to the Continent several times. I really had no idea. I got to Aberdaron because the region I wanted was north west Wales and I happened to run into some people in San Francisco who own this home that I'm renting. He's Welsh and she's American and they've owned this place for twelve years. They have six children that they always bring over in the summer for two or three months and they'd like to retire here. When I met them it was completely on impulse and they said Aberdaron is the place, you must come, and so I said yes.'

So how did Wales compare with your expectations?

'Well, I think that I'm sort of trying to find the bridge, you know? This seven, eight hundred-year bridge. So what I find is that I spend a lot of my time walking and the other part of my time studying a lot of twelfth- and thirteenth-century renderings. I mean, I can't speak Welsh so I go into the library at Bangor, at the university there, and just go through all these translated manuscripts into English and just read and research. I don't know where it's taking me, it's just a passion.

'Interestingly enough, I feel very settled here in Aberdaron and very able to do the work that I love to do. Actually, I write and I've been writing a lot since I've been here. Nothing to speak of, but between the researching and the writing there seems to be . . . I seem to relax in Wales, I seem to feel completely at home here and I don't pretend to understand it. Llŷn is very windswept, it's very dramatic, it's very green, it's studded with sheep. The pasture goes straight down to the Irish Sea on this long promontory, these cliff faces are . . . "dramatic" is the best word to describe them. And then there's Enlli sitting off, sort of hidden from Aberdaron. It acts as an anchor as far as I can tell. Part of my attraction for this area is Enlli and is the fact that back in the period that I'm so fascinated with pilgrims made a pilgrimage to Bardsey on foot down this Llŷn Peninsula and they stopped in various different parish churches. Actually Nefyn, from what I can gather had quite a large population for the time and it was because of the pilgrims on their way to

Bardsey. It's considered the isle of twenty thousand saints and before the Middle Ages it was a sacred site and it's just . . . I don't know, you just have a history in this part of the world of islands being anchors and sacred sites, and Bardsey's obviously that for this area.'

How well do you know the rest of Wales?

I don't. I've been only to the Marchland down by Hay-on-Wye. I spent about a week in that area. The Black Mountains are absolutely . . . extraordinary. And right there on the borderland there's a place called Llanthony Valley that absolutely shattered me. But other than that I really . . . I don't have a car right now so I've been very much a Llŷn Peninsula person.

'I would really love to come back. My plans are to go back to the States and spend a year or two trying to, you know, make my way back here! I'd love to learn the language and it's one of those decisions I made when I got here and started to listen to the language and thought, Oh my God, I only have five months! It would take me three or four hours every day to start to learn this language and so I didn't. If I do come back I'd like to spend at least four or five years here so that I could learn the language properly and do justice to it because I think the culture speaks through its language and I wouldn't do it justice if I didn't at least make an attempt. I'd love to read the *Mabinogion* in Welsh – my God! '

What would you hope it would give you access to?

'There's a quality in the Welsh from an outsider's point of view that is just . . . I don't know how to describe it . . . a quality of being, a quality of acceptance, a quality of things that have remained this way for centuries and will continue to remain this way. I was speaking to a friend the other day about my love affair with Wales and how I loved to walk and just be here on the land and he said, "You know," he said, "the relationship with the Welsh people and the land is one and the same. We couldn't exist without the land and the land wouldn't exist without us, would it?" It summed up that interdependence. What thrills me most is just wanting to learn more and be here longer and wanting to really understand particularly north Wales. I really had no idea it was the heart of Welsh-speaking Wales when this whole quest started. I was really sort of led here, I kind of got taken by the scruff of the neck as it were. It makes me want to have a better sense. You see, it's like layer upon layer upon layer and I've been able to pull back maybe one, maybe two, maybe three layers but there's countless others that I would love to explore.'

Brian Bessant, Llanwrtyd Wells, Powys

I follow the retreating form of a cleaner through a church doorway and meet the vicar coming out of his vestry, dressed in a plain white shirt and dark trousers with bicycle clips. Born in Gwent, Brian Bessant is currently vicar of St James'. Originally trained in fine art in Cardiff, he was ordained in the Diocese of Llandaff, served in Llangammarch, the neighbouring parish to Llanwrtyd, for five years and then moved to Crickhowell. After three years in Cyprus, he returned to Crickhowell and then to his present position. He is an iconographer in the Byzantine tradition, working on commissions for a wide range of churches, although his own church contains no examples. We talk sitting on the pews of this airy, late Victorian church while around us a small band of volunteers arrange flowers.

'I come from a Nonconformist background and the tradition locally tends to be Nonconformist and I'm happy to fit in with that. But I love Orthodoxy as well although I wouldn't give offence to people by doing something only because I personally found it helpful.

'I see this as my last incumbency. I'm very happy to think of spending the next twelve or however many years it may be here working on a series of icons for this church.

'I trained in art college for six years. The call to ordination arose – as with many people – out of a vow to God. I'd always had this sort of chapel and Sunday school background. Even when I was in art college I remember deciding that I would offer myself to, at the time, the Presbyterian Church of Wales. But by that time really, I was moving. In art college I had made contact with the curate of St John's in Cardiff. It was just little things, really; but I found the fact that we didn't kneel in the Presbyterian Church very difficult. I wanted to kneel. When I went to see Glyn Simon, who was then the Bishop of Llandaff, to discuss being ordained into the Church in Wales, he said two things: "You will need theological training," and, "you'd better start going to church!"'

What part does iconography play in your own spirituality?

'I find it's this sense of entering into the understanding of the Church which is so important for me. But it's not a personal thing. I'm not on an ego trip. That's what most artists are about, but I'm not doing that. Your contribution towards it is almost unconscious . . . I am liberated by it; I don't feel in any way suppressed by it. I think if my only aim was to make my own individual contribution, it would in the end be a very mean thing, because as an individual I am a very small person.'

What role does the Church in Wales perform in the life of Wales?

'It's very different from town to country. In the country it still does have a community focus. It's a source of cohesion. The chapels are in rapid decline, and although the church here was never terribly well attended, the old parish church on the outskirts of Llanwrtyd Wells is still considered to be the parish church by members of Bethesda Calvinistic Methodist church and of the Congregational church because they have relatives buried there. We have a united service there once a year. People come very happily. I've inherited the mantle of those who went before me. And I go into school. I'm always welcome in the school. It's an ordinary state school, but I go there normally once a week and take the assembly. I ride with them once a week, too. I'm a community person and I think my role is to be part of this community . . . Things are well here. We have difficulties, but things are basically well. It's an extraordinarily generous community. Everything that happens here is well supported. People who come in tell you that they can't understand just how active the community is and how busy it is. There's always something to do. It may well be because it grows out of tourism. Although it's on the edge of Welsh Wales, Llanwrtyd has been geared to tourism from the middle of the last century, when the railways came. At that time it depended upon having wealthy families coming here with their servants, taking over the hotels and the boarding houses. That disappeared at the end of the First World War. Then you had day trips – or what we called fortnight trips – from the Valleys, which flowed in during the summer. People will tell you locally that through the summer their would be a thousand visitors a week here, in a town with a population of six hundred, so that the people here would be constantly outnumbered throughout the summer months. And people who were not local would tell you that you could not, on a summer evening, even cycle through the streets here because the overflow from the chapels was such that there simply wasn't room for traffic. It was a very vibrant place in the summer months. Now that's all gone – we have bus trips that come and stay, just briefly, at the Abernant Lake on tours of Wales. After the last War trekking became very strong. Now that's been joined by mountain biking and it's taking over walking as well. The forestry trails are ideal for that sort of thing. As part of my work here I take parties of young children out along those trails.'

As we are leaving Brian Bessant remarks that it was at the old parish church that the Welsh hymn writer Pantycelyn served a curacy. From his own chapel upbringing he can sympathise, he says, with Pantycelyn's description of nonconformity as 'a raven stealing bright things'. Celtic Christianity had more vibrancy. In one rural Welsh parish a vicar is seeking to restore something of that spiritual energy.

Joseph Biddulph, Pontypridd, Mid Glamorgan

Joseph Biddulph is forty-four and was born in Handsworth, Birmingham. He studied English Literature at University College Aberystwyth. After teacher training and two years in East Anglia, he moved to Pontypridd to take a teaching job in Cardiff. Between us, on a low table, lies a pile of booklets on the grammar and accidence of Lithuanian, Yoruba, Ibo . . .

'I was working as a teacher until the end of 1979, when I thought it was about time for a change because I didn't get on with the job particularly, but I found that the first of the Great Recessions was on at the time, so I didn't get a job. So as a way out of unemployment, I thought, well I'll pursue this self-employment thing, see what I can offer in the way of my talents to the public at large. And that's really how I got into the languages thing. I mostly publish: I publish booklets with a great emphasis on the obscurer languages, but covering other subjects as well. For instance, the little thing on Lithuanian. Now, I was a very unwilling self-taught student of Lithuanian, made very little progress in my mind, but I decided I'd summarise what results I'd got in the form of a booklet. And lo and behold, it's the only one in print at a reasonable price on Lithuanian! And I've had an obsession with African languages, which is probably unusual for someone who's never set foot in the place, and one of the things I've tried to do – and tried to get other people interested in – is to try and explore some of the enormous variety there is. And I've brought out a booklet from time to time on . . . well, some of them were obscure, but to my mind nearly every African language is obscure because it's very very difficult to get material on them. It is as if they don't exist, which is a great pity. So I've tried to explore other areas as well. I'm keen on Anglo Saxon, Old Germanic and what have you. But once again I found that some of the little things I managed to get out were sort of unique in their type. Surprisingly, the little summary I did of Old Saxon turned out to be one of the few things people can actually get their hands on. I've got the sort of mind that goes after the unusual.'

And what about Welsh?

'Well, I'm a bit of a failure in this respect. I don't think I'm much of a Celticist. I read Welsh. I've even written Welsh, but I don't speak the language. I don't live in an area where Welsh is widely spoken, so if you want to speak Welsh in Pontypridd you have to seek out Welsh-speaking company. It's a funny relationship with the Welsh language because at one time I thought the one thing I wanted in all the world was to be able to speak Welsh really well. But when I was canvassing for Plaid Cymru and later became a candidate for the local council, I knocked on the doors and people said, "Oh, I don't want to vote for you because you'll be forcing the Welsh language down people's throats. Just because you can speak Welsh . . . " And I could say, with my hand on my heart, "I'm sorry, I don't speak Welsh. I'm not even Welsh, I'm English." The emphasis got deflected into politics for a while and . . . well, I pursue the Welsh language as an interest, as a literary interest. People think that's a bit strange – "How many languages do you speak?" they say – but it's something I'm interested in, something I've had an interest in since I was about twelve, I think.'

How do you find Pontypridd?

'I have a memory of Pontypridd when I lived in Aberystwyth, coming through on the coach from Cardiff, stopping just opposite the church where I worship now and saying, "What a horrible place. How can anyone bear to live here?" Which is something I have gone back on many a time since. I can't really complain. I'm within twelve miles of the capital city; anything that goes on in Wales will come to this end sooner or later; I've hob-nobbed with all sorts of interesting people, and yet there's a mountain either side of our street, there's open moorland within a few minutes' walk. You've got the best of both worlds, really. You've got a railway running down the middle of the valley, lots of stations and a frequent service, frequent bus services, but at the same time you've got all this open countryside, something that people just don't know about the Valleys, lots of landscape.

People pass right through Pontypridd, straight up the trunk road to go to the Brecon Beacons, not realising they're missing out some very spectacular scenery.

'I've lived here longer than I've lived anywhere else and you get a sort of loyalty. I went away during the summer for a couple of days and I got so bad that I was glad to be back again: I got that personal experience of what *hiraeth* is. The family are very much Welsh and with Welsh sympathies by now. They certainly wouldn't want me to pick up stumps now and say right, I want to go to Worcestershire or somewhere. So it looks as if I'm here. It's something I feel a commitment to, of course, because I do know the society so well after all these years it's something that I think I can understand and I think I know how it ticks. If I was anywhere else I'd be a stranger; I'd just have to learn all the ropes again from the beginning.

'On the positive side, the great unsung resource of Wales is the people – particularly the Valleys, particularly south Wales, where you get this spontaneous generosity. When we moved to this house we had nothing. Within a few minutes we had a table and a chair and a cooking stove given to us by people we'd never seen or met before. That's an example of the sort of spontaneous generosity that people have: they see into other people's problems and sympathise with them. Of course, on the down side, there's the fact that people seem to have too great a curiosity about other people's affairs, which to me, coming from a big city, is something I still find difficulty with. And a certain amount of petty persecution. They like persecuting people for . . . well, I was thinking of some of the youngsters around this area, for being different in some way. There have been times when I've thought, well this place is just the pits and I'd much rather live anywhere. I've thought, the petty-mindedness, the narrow-mindedness of people, in public life or whatever. Their visions seem so low all the time. That's something that's maybe the same everywhere, but it certainly contributes to the down side. I want to name names here, but I'd better not . . . I'm thinking in terms of the Welsh cringe, right? I'll give you an example. There was a local protest group about starting up a cement works. Everybody was against it; everybody was dead keen that they were going to prevent it. When I suggested to the meeting that they should invite the Secretary of State for Wales personally to the next meeting – even if he refused, we'd have done it and all the rest of it – they all said, "Oh, we can't do that yet. We've got to get powerful people around us." And to me that seems unambitious. They seemed to be giving up the fight before they'd even started. And then there's the way that certain people in public life seem to be wanting to build an empire for themselves as if they don't feel really a person unless they're VIPs, unless they've got people saying how wonderful they are, what great contributions they're making, blah, blah, blah. I find all that very galling, because my concept of public life is more service, responding to real needs rather than blowing my own trumpet all the time.

'I've done things like serve on the Citizens' Advice Bureau and on the Community Health Council. One thing I think is very important at the moment is the Credit Union movement. I'm one of the founding members, if I can put it like that, of the first community Credit Union in Wales. It's something that I'm very enthusiastic about because I see it as a solution to the problems of poverty and so on. We've got over two hundred members. The background is that although Rhydfelen, this end of Pontypridd, is a big area – what you might call a suburb I suppose – the heart of the Credit Union is the priority estate at Glyntaff Farm and the people most involved are the tenants and residents there. In a few years you've turned round what was a very low-status, hopeless kind community into one which is actually looking to itself, looking after its own affairs and seeking fresh ways of emancipating itself. We're talking about somewhere that's among the most deprived areas in Western Europe; we're talking about high unemployment; we're talking about broken families; we're talking about people labouring under all kinds of social disadvantages. We've got currently about £50,000 out in the community which just wouldn't be there if it wasn't for the Credit Union. It's like every other association: you've got a handful of stalwarts who guide it through.

'I've been struck ever since I've been in this area by the number of English people in particular who've got involved in things. I'm in the Inter-Church group and when I was in Birmingham it was commonplace for clergy to come from South Wales. But in Pontypridd it's completely the other way around and if you get any new clergy coming in, usually with fresh ideas, they're usually from England somewhere. And you find out that often you can't tell straightway because they've been living in the area for a number of years and they know the ropes and a bit of the dialect. But you often find the people who are working hard in certain areas are the Anglo Saxons. It may be a terrible thing to say, but there we are (!) They've been here for a long time and they've become virtually naturalised.'

How naturalised do you feel?

'It varies. Sometimes when people are talking about "in" things I feel like an outsider. But on other occasions I sort of rejoice because I feel I'm actually part of it, particularly the wisecracks and the jokes. You've got a roomful of people and they're all knocking spots off one another in the most good-natured sort of way and suddenly I'm in there and I'm with them and if somebody came in who was fresh from England or something – perhaps a bit stiff, not connecting with the anarchic sense of humour – I'd think, Oh well, I'm one of these, you know; me, I'm naturalised!

'I'll give you an illustration of that. Last summer I went down to Eastbourne to visit relations. But in order to do it the interesting fashion I travelled by local bus over a couple of days rather than by train. And when you travel by bus you get a feel for the local community. And as I was going from south Wales, the further and further away I went the more and more alien and cold the place was. When I was down in Sussex the people were sitting on the buses with straight backs, exchanging platitudes, very-warm-today-isn't-it sort of thing. There was a completely different sort of feel. I felt as if I was among foreigners. It was an unsympathetic environment. Well, I was coming back and I got on the bus in Bristol that goes to

Chepstow, but it calls in a lot of villages on the way. And suddenly the whole bus was alive. There were all these women at the back and they were all talking away at once and I thought, they sound as if they're Welsh. Sure enough, they all stayed on the bus till we got over the Bridge to Chepstow. The feeling I had when I got on that bus was warmth and I felt I was coming home. I got on the next bus in Chepstow, the driver was probably from Newport or somewhere, and he looked and his gestures and everything else were different. You could say anything to him. You can't say anything to an English bus-driver – you just ask for the fare and that's about it. But he was eager to open up and he was voluble and he was talkative. There was that volubility that I'd missed when I was away in foreign parts, so to speak.'

Cefin Campbell, Llandeilo, Dyfed*

Cefin is thirty-five and has been involved with Menter Cwm Gwendraeth *since its inception three years ago. Funded by the Welsh Office, it is a pioneering community project aimed at fostering the Welsh language in an semi-industrial valley on the borders of West Glamorgan and the former Carmarthenshire. We have made an appointment to meet at the Eisteddfod and now I am late, as inevitably happens, hurrying across the field. I find him concluding a conversation with a woman from the BBC World Service where he has just completed another interview.*

'I come from the Amman Valley originally, a very industrial area itself of course. When I was a very young lad I was familiar with seeing miners coming and going, working different shifts; that was a very common sight. Well, by now the Valley is suffering dreadfully from the effects of the recession and unemployment and I believe that the Valleys generally, including the Gwendraeth where I work at present, are suffering and that means that there's a lack of confidence amongst people and that reflects itself in their confidence in the language, which is something I naturally worry about very much. On average the number of Welsh speakers in Cwm Gwendraeth is around seventy-five per cent. There are pockets of Welsh higher than that; Pontyberem parish, for example, and Cross Hands at over eighty. Certainly, as regards the number of Welsh speakers, this is the biggest area in Wales. There are higher percentages in other places, but as far as the size of population who can speak the language goes, this is the biggest.

'What we realised from the outset is that we can't divorce language from community and we've been working as part of a very wide strategy to run language campaigns, projects to promote the use of the language, raising the profile of the language alongside movements to reduce unemployment, offering training to young people, new skills for young people and additionally of course things like housing and planning and improving the environment. It's all part of the process of creating a new life for people, a more valuable quality of life where people believe that they belong and want to live in their communities.

'Very roughly I'd say that Cwm Gwendraeth is about twenty miles square and includes around thirty-five thousand people, quite a populous area to be honest. There are some very large villages here, like Cross Hands and Tumble for example. As regards staff, there are four of us full-time; there's a whole host of volunteers and we depend on them extensively and we're very grateful to them for all their assistance. The four of us find it hard to meet all the demands because when we have a success with individual projects there are other areas within the Cwm where people want to see something similar, or different age groups wanting to see more provision for them, but even as this snowball gathers pace and grows we're still only the same number of staff. The pressures on our energy and time are huge. I'd like to have more . . .

'There are a vast number of projects, ranging from things like concerts, folk nights . . . and we have *Gŵyl y Gwendraeth*, a big festival every year. A committee of about fifteen people work together to prepare it year after year, and within this committee there are particular interests: the musical side, sports side, children and young people, nursery-age children – they all have an important contribution to make. Then there are projects concerned with the environment which bring other people in, projects in the schools which bring in teachers. The teachers have been very, very supportive and, of course, the teachers are very grateful to the *Fenter* because although they make a splendid contribution, their hours as teachers are restricted; they work between nine and half past three, and of course what's been happening to the children and the children's language after half past three, the teachers have been losing control of that. I'm trying now to provide for these young people outside school hours to reinforce what's taught in school as far as language goes.

'The Welsh Office and the Welsh Language Board wanted to see whether the model of a language project like this could work. We're in the process at present of trying to convince the Board – and I don't think that it will be a difficult thing for us to do – that there is a future and that there's an important role for language ventures. We have seen that we can convince people in their communities, in their homes, as individuals even, that the language is something very valuable to us as Welsh people, and raise consciousness and change attitudes and at the end of the day give them the confidence to use it.'

How can success be measured?

'That's a huge and very difficult task, something that we're trying to come to terms with at present. We do have an appraisal process as a *Menter* for particular projects. On a more general level, are we succeeding in changing the linguistic course of the Cwm? That's the big question. I don't believe perhaps that even in my lifetime that we'll see the . . . fruits of our labours, but we are very confident because of very small examples and we believe that by putting them together that that can change patterns of language, that there's change afoot. Can I give you an example? When the *Fenter* started, in the social clubs – what they call the "workies", very popular places, extremely sociable places, the rugby clubs the same – the entertainment was in English. They saw that as something normal, getting artists from the English circuit of course, and that worked to some extent. But when we started to introduce Welsh artists, entertainment through the medium of Welsh, they saw three things happen straightaway: one, a growth in their audience; two, their coffers were fuller; and the third thing was more publicity through the *Fenter* for their individual club because we gave assistance with that side of things. The result is that the clubs now use Welsh artists, use a Welsh programme, use Welsh publicity, and that's a success that can be measured.'

How stable is the population of Cwm Gwendraeth?

'Well, there are two valleys in Cwm Gwendraeth. Not many people are aware of that. There's the Gwendraeth Fach and the Gwendraeth Fawr, and Gwendraeth Fach is a beautiful, rural valley, the one that they wanted to drown back in the sixties.

And that valley's seen a lot of incomers during the last decade. Over the years it was a static population that saved the Welsh language in Gwendraeth and Amman, too. Workers from the neighbouring Welsh-speaking valleys who came into the area to work in the coalmines stayed there as long as there was work for them. Now the mines have all closed and young people have to look for work elsewhere. It's not available in Cwm Gwendraeth: unemployment is around the twenty per cent mark. What we are seeing is emigration, especially young people, young people who are Welsh speakers. It is they who will be, or they would have been, the natural leaders of the community. Their children would have filled the nurseries and the local schools with their Welsh. They're going in droves because there's a shortage of work here and that's a source of great concern to me.

'I believe that the Cwm over the last few years has realised that something important and very precious is being lost. They've seen huge changes in a world where there was work for everybody, where local pubs and shops thrived. They're closed now. They see their children leaving the area, they see their children going to the colleges and unable to get jobs back in the area. They see this opencasting ravaging the environment. They see houses for sale everywhere and nobody buying them. They see ruins; they see the ruination of a community around them. And they realise that they have perhaps placed too much faith in the political order and they realise now that the power is in their hands at the end of the day, that it's in the hands of the people themselves to rebuild community. I hope that the *Fenter* plays a part, along with other movements of course, in achieving that aim of rebuilding the confidence and rebuilding a future for us in Cwm Gwendraeth.'

He brings both palms down onto the table with businesslike finality. Around us families struggle past the open tent flap.

W. Elwyn Conway, Rhyl, Clwyd

Elwyn Conway was born in Rhyl. He has spent over half of his sixty-nine years involved in local government at borough and county level and considers himself to be 'a reasonable observer of the general scene'. We speak in the deserted function room of the town's Labour Club.

'I've travelled throughout Wales and I've come to the conclusion that Wales, being the country it is with the type of people it has, ought to have its own identity by way of an elected, democratically accountable Welsh assembly to get away from the unfair and undue influences of central government in London. I'm quite sure that there are sufficient personalities in the Principality to make a far better job of government at all levels and control of all the undemocratic quangos by properly, directly accountable representatives who can be hired and fired at the will of the electorate and that this is true democracy.'

Would Wales still sent representatives to Westminster?

'If there were to be a federal structure and it came to be that as part of the United Kingdom, so-called, Wales had to be represented, yes, there'd be nothing wrong with that. No more than there's anything wrong with representation now in Europe, which under present circumstances has been for some years the salvation of areas like Wales from the domination that has meant Wales being downgraded in regional development and welfare. In all kinds of ways Wales has come off second-best, really. The real solution is part of a wider picture – and all the regions of Europe feel this way as well – they should have a regional identity within a wider community that can and does, despite its beaurocracy, have a set-up that allows for regional expression of thought, that can be taken to the centre and given proper account and not have, as now exists in the U.K., a Wales being treated separately from the rest of the United Kingdom. The classic example of that is the current reorganisation of local government. Wales has been dealt with directly and absolutely differently from the rest of the United Kingdom. The

Government are denying the expression of Welsh interest in an elected Welsh assembly, their insistence being that we are part of a United Kingdom. But the treatment is different. In England a commission has been set up under John Banham which has been taking evidence and trying to come up with a solution to so-called perceived weaknesses of the last reorganisation, which incidentally was presided over by the same Government, the Conservative Government of 1974. The then Secretary of State for the Environment was a chap called Peter Walker- he is now lording it up in the Upper House – and he introduced local government then and said it was the finest thing that ever happened and would last well into the next century. As we know, that hasn't proved to be the case, but there have been no local ministerial resignations. And now the mistakes are to be ironed out, so we're told, but we're not having the benefit of a commission like Sir John Banham's in England. We're really subject to central government diktat. And a lot of people in Wales – and this is because Wales has its own expression of democracy through the ballot box whereby we are not in favour of the landed gentry, the right wing privileged set – we happen to elect representatives of a different political persuasion, the overwhelming number being Labour. The Government see this as something they must spitefully tackle by diktat, expressed through guide-lines and all sorts of things from London. It means that we've been dealt with differently here and it's an order of the Welsh Office, compounded by . . . the monarch having given Royal Assent to this happening here in Wales. So although we're part of the United Kingdom and the Queen rules over us, happy and glorious, according to the thing we have to sing from time to time, we're being dealt with separately to the rest of her subjects, and in a diabolical, wicked, undemocratic way. I've taken exception to this and I expressed myself in the most forceful terms at the Assembly of Welsh County Council representatives in Cardiff. They had before them reports, independent reports, which absolutely contradict some of the lunatic assumptions made by Government ministers who say what will be good for Wales. They're making assumptions which are absolutely at odds with professional opinion. Indeed,

I went so far as to strongly urge members that Her Majesty ought to be acquainted with the effects on the people of Wales of the reorganisation that she has blessed. If she's given assent – and consent – to people in Wales being treated differently to people in other parts of the country, then I think she and her advisers ought to be looking at this. Because we have no hope with this Government. It has its majority, treating minorities with total contempt and arrogance. The cost of reorganisation is going to be astronomical and the effect is going to be picked up by the communities, because within the existing level of local government expenditure are to be borne the costs of this reorganisation and that will mean a further attack by way of cutback in local services, and the biggest recipient of local services are those most in need. This means an attack on Her Majesty's subjects: elderly people, and at the other end of the scale, young people in education.

'I've been in the Labour Party all my life and I want them to be electable. If they're not perceived to be electable and no-one will elect them, then it's no use sitting around tables pontificating about what might or what can happen. They really need to be in a position to deliver and if that's the case they need to make themselves accountable and be identified with the needs of the masses . . . This is a very complex, comprehensive problem to deal with, and it will take some years, but the sooner we get a different type of government to the one we have had since 1979, the sooner I think that will be brought about . . . We need to look at society as a whole, create a happy society. A utopian dream if you like, but if we don't have dreams and hopes and aspirations, what have we?'

For the first time during our conversation Elwyn Conway allows himself a faint smile.

Diane Cooper, Builth Wells, Powys

Diane Cooper is forty-seven and a native of Aberystwyth. She has been in the licensed trade ten years. She and her husband run the White Horse Inn in Builth, popular with locals and foreign visitors who stay in its nine beds.

'I went to school in Aberystwyth. I suppose as a teenager I thought it was a bit of a dead-end place, you know. All my friends went to London, it was a big thing to do then, but looking back I suppose Aberystwyth was a wonderful place to grow up. It was very quiet. There was no night-life as such, but having said that, it was pretty safe to walk the streets as well, which there's a lot to be said for.'

And night-life in Builth?

'Pubs. That's it, that is it. We don't have a Tescos or a Woolworths or anything, we've just got the pubs. At this time of the year it's tourists, mainly tourists. The locals, they work hard and they play hard, but they don't go out till the weekend. Usually. Unless it's very hot – most of them are forestry workers and farmers – and then they probably come out for a couple later on.

'Business brought us over here. We used to have a pub in Ludlow which was a total disaster. We went back to Aberystwyth then and we didn't work for about six months and then this came up as a tenanted house eight years ago so we came to have a look at it and took it on. Then about four years ago we had the option of buying or getting out – with the Monopoly Commission, you know – so we decided that, being as we liked the town and we knew the trade, that we'd take it on. I like the area. On the whole the Welsh are very friendly . . . they're very nosy, they're very friendly and if ever you're in trouble they're great. It's a great community, that sort of thing, it's good. Originally my husband's from Shropshire, but that's bordering on Wales and he's probably about fifteen years in Wales so he's adopted.'

Have you been hit by the recession?

'Not particularly, but then again we don't get hit by the boom either. You know, the tidal wave sort of runs out just before it gets here. It's neither good nor bad. I mean, the only thing that's good for us here is the Royal Welsh showground. It brings a lot of trade in, a lot of trade. . . and if it's not with accommodation it's with food and drink. We do a lot of food, particularly if there's a couple of days' events on the showground. A lot of them will camp and then come out for food, but we don't pick it up in bed and breakfast. That's hit us a little bit, things like pony sales and sheep sales. Whereas before they'd come and stay . . . it's hit us there. But having said that, they all come out and eat of an evening. It's pretty good, pretty good, but there again it's very quiet in the winter. The last couple of years we've had a lot of construction workers with one thing and another and – touch wood – we've done very well over the winter months. What will happen this year I don't know, but when you've got three bedrooms full for three months at a time you don't moan about it.

Have you noticed any changes in Builth over the last eight years?

'I don't think it has changed. The only thing that worries me is they want to put a by-pass through here, around here, and I think that'll make a hell of a difference to the place. On our side of the fence, we don't want it. On the general householder side, I don't think they realise the effects . . . I know it's a pain to have heavy lorries going through the town, but if they have a by-pass it's going to kill the town, I think, totally. What a lot of them don't realise – a lot of them have got jobs in the shops – and if we're not spending the money around the town then they're going to lose their jobs. As I say, I agree, it's a pain the heavy traffic, but you've seen it around the area . . . Llanidloes is a prime example. They've got a by-pass there and I go there for meat and it's like a ghost town. I mean, nobody's going to go off the dual carriageway to find a pub for a meal. They'll drive on to the next car park sort of thing. Welshpool have done it;

Newtown is in the process of doing it, Llanidloes have done it and I suppose it's progress, but I don't know. It's actually been shelved at the moment – apparently it's still in the Welsh Office. I honestly think if that was on the cards I'd get out of it, because I don't think you can survive on the local trade totally, you know you need the tourists. I wouldn't leave Builth, but I'd leave the trade.

'We have a livestock market, but that's another thing at the moment, they're talking about moving it to Brecon. They've talked about this for a couple of years and it hasn't happened, so whether it will I don't know.'

Does Builth have quite a stable population?

'It's pretty stable. You tend to find that the majority of the youngsters will stay here, they won't move away. In the farming community there is work, the other main thing is forestry and then in the area there are small factory units. There's a very small industrial estate here, but there's quite a big one in Llandrindod, which is seven miles away and there's quite a few people work there. There's a couple of places up there actually, there's a pine factory, there's a carpet factory, there's a bookbinders – that takes quite a few of our people. Then we've got a big sawmill just up the road which takes quite a few – it's very steady, so I can't see them closing in the foreseeable future.'

At this point a group of young Spaniards arrive, ordering lager, pointing at the jukebox. The bar is filled, incongruously, with the strains of 'I've Got a Brand New Combine Harvester'. Conversation becomes impossible. Diana Cooper wipes away the wet rings on her bar.

Aled Davies, Pontyberem, Dyfed*

Aled Davies is twenty-five, a native of Menai Bridge and, since October 1993, Chair of Cymdeithas yr Iaith, *the Welsh Language Society, which he joined in his early teens. After graduating at University College Cardiff, he worked as tutor-organiser in Welsh as a second language for University College Swansea, covering Llanelli and the Amman and Gwendraeth Valleys. We are talking at the Eisetddfod in an empty tent under a banner saying Bwrdd yr Iaith, the Welsh Language Board, part of the Cymdeithas protest at the Language Board's failure to have a stand there. By the end of our conversation a small crowd of inquisitive onlookers has gathered. Has a representative of the Board broken cover?*

How did your connection with Cymdeithas yr Iaith start?

'It was just seeing in my everyday experience that the Welsh language was under siege and in danger of disappearing as a living language. In the town where I was brought up about two thirds of the population spoke Welsh, so there was a living Welsh language community there, but at the same time there were a number of people with no Welsh, so there was an awareness that the community was being eroded to some extent. The threat to the language was very alive there. It wasn't a place where the language was completely secure nor where Welsh had died out as a living language either and I suppose that my awareness of the position of the language developed as I became more active.

'Since the early days of the Gymdeithas there have been very definite changes in our campaigns. There's more realisation now that, essentially, we must look not just at purely linguistic factors such as the status of the language on road signs, the status of the language in council offices, banks, whatever; that it's not just a matter of seeing the language enjoying equal status with English – although that is important – but that we must look at more basic things which affect the communities that sustain the language. The economic and social factors . . .

political factors such as how communities are run. The Gymdeithas sees now that to secure the future of the language we must support the communities of Wales and that those communities must have the opportunity and the freedom to develop, that an economy be allowed to develop that's favourable to their continuation. There must be structures in place so that communities can take control of their own future, so that people feel part of their community. After fifteen years of Tory rule, these are ideas which have certainly been eroded in England and to some extent in Wales, too. These are things that we have to fight for.'

If Cymdeithas yr Iaith plays a political role, can it be placed within the conventional political spectrum?

'I suppose we're partly socialist. There's not much doubt about that. We're also nationalist to the extent that we feel that Wales is a national unit. But it's not a matter of ensuring that Wales is an independent country run in the same way that Britain is currently run as an independent country. It's more a matter of developing a system of government that can answer community needs. And in that respect I suppose green politics comes into it, too. For example, members of the Gymdeithas have been lending their support to the protest in Wales against opencast mining, because opencast, apart from the fact that it's environmentally damaging, is something that eats into communities. It's not just realising that a big black hole in the back garden is unpleasant for the locals, it's realising that it's something that's destroying these areas. There's a huge slice of south Wales liable to affected. Whether it's private enterprise or British Coal, they can damage communities, and not only environmentally. In some areas they're buying property in huge blocks, targeting them, buying them out.

'My impression is that we have more members now who are committed to the Gymdeithas than before. Not just people going through some phase before moving on to pastures new. But the majority of the members are still young. A large proportion of our members are school and college students, people around that age-group.'

In the seventies the successes of the Gymdeithas in raising the public profile of Welsh were more visible. Is it still possible to feel a sense of achievement?

'We still have some successes like that. A number of building societies have recently adopted bilingual policies because of the work of the Gymdeithas. Some other achievements have come about constitutionally. We won – partially at least – the battle for a body to develop Welsh language education. The gains aren't so obvious now, that's true, but there's a growing awareness of the needs of Welsh and support for, or a consciousness of, the aims of the Gymdeithas spreading within and outside institutions. That in itself is a victory.'

I switch off the machine and Aled exhales dramatically. 'Did that make sense?' he asks. 'You know, you get talking like that and you don't know what you're saying.' For perhaps the only time in the course of the summer an interviewee reaches out and shakes my hand.

Bryan Davies, Brecon, Powys

Bryan Davies is fifty-five and a native of Brecon, where his family have lived continuously for 'four or five hundred years'. He left school at sixteen and joined the RAF a year later. He served for twenty-two years and then left to take up a post at the Jobcentre in Caerffili before being transferred to Brecon. He worked in the Brecon office for fifteen years and is now semi-retired. Ironically, we met at the same Jobcentre, where Bryan is now seeking part-time work for himself. He understands unemployment professionally and now personally.

'I think that the main problem in Brecon is that over the years we've had factories move in to pick up the grants that were available at the time and brought people with them. And those firms have now either moved away or gone bust and the people who were working in them have been left behind. And there's a large number of ex-servicemen settled here – that has always been the case because this is a military town – who, I think, find it difficult to readjust to civilian life and don't have the necessary skills. There's also a large number of people like myself who haven't reached full retirement age yet, but need to keep their credits going, need to sign. And altogether that's a significant number of people. I think I remember that when I was working here Brecon had the highest percentage of people unemployed for over twelve months between fifty-five and sixty of anywhere in Wales. It's very much a retirement area. Property is not cheap in Brecon, but it's a lot cheaper than some other parts of the country. People have sold up in the south-east of England, moved here and the chances of them getting employment at fifty-five at anything like the wages they were getting before – because wages tend to be low anyway in this part of the world – well, it's a little difficult for them.'

Are most job vacancies in the service sector?

'Yes, hotel and catering form a large percentage, but also the statutory bodies like the hospitals, the Ministry of Defence obviously and things like the local Co-op. I remember when the new Co-op was built here in Brecon, it seemed to be a little bit of a watershed. It seemed to bring in a lot . . . but I don't think that if they built another on the outskirts of town it would do any good at all. Leominster is a town very similar to Brecon and they built one there and the centre of Leominster's dead. There's been talk of a development just off the road to Merthyr but I think that's been knocked on the head now. What Brecon needs is some responsible development within the town. There's been a big dispute going on for years about the Bethel area – a disused chapel in the centre of town. The interior's gone and it's just deteriorated and deteriorated, because nobody will make a decision, nobody will say, right we'll go ahead and do something. It's just a disused chapel and a row of disused cottages which used to be very pretty. The whole area needs sorting out. There is a project to build an inner ring road that might help relieve the traffic, but I don't know if that's what Brecon really needs. It certainly needs something.

'Being in the National Park doesn't help. I know I'm being very Welsh about this . . . I think that it has put so many restrictions on development. For example, when this office was built they refused to let us have "Jobcentrē" in large letters on it and yet they stipulated on the plans that the flowerbed had a eucalyptus in it. Now, I can understand having a mountain ash which is a native plant . . . In some ways they're good, they're responsible professional people, but I think they're not responsible enough to local people. I think that anybody who's on the board of the National Park should have to live in the National Park and they should be elected by people who live in the National Park. There'd be some local responsibility then, and accountability.

'I know a lot of local hotels and publicans . . . when you go into a French town, on the outskirts, there's a little green cross, like a noticeboard, saying when they hold the church services and you'll see a list of the hotels that are in the town and whether they're one star or two star or three star, this sort of thing. Now that would help the local traders, but the National Parks won't allow that sort of thing. Understandably in some ways because you can get overkill, but if it's done in a responsible way and thought out then it can only help the town.

'The other thing that a lot of local people are upset about is that we've had a new leisure centre built. OK, wonderful, but it's right at the top of a hill, quite a steep hill, three quarters of a mile out of town. It's right next to the school with no playing fields and that's fine, but what happens is they get a development grant for it and when that money's gone the local residents are going to have to pay for it. If it's not used enough it means the rates are going to have to pay for it or something, but the local residents aren't using it . . . it's the visitors. And that's happening all over Wales. I feel that the developers are moving in and the money is coming from the EC to develop, but the money isn't going to local people, it's going to big firms from England who get the contracts, who bring in the labour so it doesn't affect the local labour field, and then they go and we're left with, in some cases, white elephants.'

Bryan Davies thanks me for allowing him 'to get that off my chest'. As I leave the jobcentre I can see him surveying a board of white cards headed 'Miscellaneous'.

David Wynn Davies, Trelawnyd, Rhyl, Clwyd

David Wynn Davies is thirty-six. He was born and brought up in Dyserth and has worked as an Entertainments and Recreation Officer for Rhuddlan Borough Council for the past six years, having previously worked with the neighbouring borough of Delyn. His area of responsibility covers the coast from Prestatyn to the west of Rhyl and inland as far as Bodfari, Rhuddlan itself, St Asaph, Dyserth and Meliden. He speaks here in a personal capacity.

'I work in the main tourist areas of Rhyl and Prestatyn although we're obviously conscious that because we're here to encourage the residents of the Borough to participate in sports and recreation, it's important that we also go into the rural areas and promote sport and recreation there as well.'

Is there a tension between meeting local need and satisfying the demands of tourism?

'It's always a fine balance. We perhaps differ from a lot of local authorities in that a lot of the capital investment within the Borough goes towards tourism-related projects. Hence we've got a multi-million pound redevelopment on the Promenade in Rhyl: the new events arena, a brand new Children's Village and in the future a new marina. We've also got new developments in Prestatyn. Now, because of the economic situation within the Borough we rely heavily on tourism, so hopefully we will be up among the most advanced resorts in the twenty-first century.

'We've had to, however, be conscious that all the residents of the Borough do require from us a slice of that cake. They need to have some benefits from my Section. Rather than just do events and activities like roadshows or sporting tournaments which are tourism-related, we also have to cater for the demands of the rural areas, so we do try and organise events and recreational activities for them as well. We were conscious about three or four years ago that most of our energies were directed to the main towns, so we looked at introducing an It's A Knockout. It's an inter-village competition where we chose about twenty different sports and asked teams from all the smaller towns and the rural villages within the Borough to provide a team – and we deliberately excluded Rhyl and Prestatyn from the event. And it's a successful event. It attracts a lot of people from the various villages who don't regularly participate in sport. With some of the sports, like badminton and tennis, we found that people perhaps haven't lifted a racquet in maybe fifteen, twenty years. But because the local team manager has twisted their arm they've said, "Well, oh, all right, because it's you we'll participate", and they've not only enjoyed it on the day, but they've actually taken up the sport – which is the object of the exercise. It also encourages community spirit. We've found that as you get more and more housing developments and everybody seems to have at least one car, the old village community spirit was on the decline . . . people not knowing each other. And we found that when the team manager raises a team it does bring a lot of spirit and *hwyl* to the actual village. They come together, they practise on a weekly basis, they have a sense of belonging which perhaps a few years ago was lost. So we've found that this kind of inter-village competition is a success. Fortunately we get sponsorship from one of the major supermarket chains and it's held for one day, in October usually, and it is a roaring success. It's in its fourth year now.'

How did you set about finding local team managers?

'That is the crux of the whole problem. Really we as a Borough Recreation Section organise it, but the organisation is the easy bit. It's getting the team members together which is the difficulty, so we have had problems in finding team managers who've been prepared to sacrifice a lot of time, a lot of their time spent with phone calls. We chose team managers who were well known in their individual communities and had an ability or an inclination towards organising various sporting activities. We've been very, very fortunate. We've found the right managers in the right locations. It's difficult for them, especially when you come to the more rural areas, where due to the size of the particular villages – they're so small that in fact they're hamlets – we've combined the teams. Now, the team manager may well live in the village of Tremeirchion and may not have as many connections in the neighbouring village of Cwm or Bodfari. So, although the actual rural team comprises four or five different hamlets, the tendency is that the bulk of the team members comes from one village, which is natural really. But we have about fifty-plus members in each team and we've deliberately targeted the sports to each age group. So for the young we'll have uni-hoc, but we'll also have indoor bowls, perhaps, for the older generation. So we do have a good cross-section of the community and from all walks of life.

'Initially we were asked to go out into the community to demonstrate some of the games, which we did willingly. We'd go out maybe on a summer's evening, on a Thursday night, and the team manager will have got a team together and we will have demonstrated games like volleyball or uni-hoc or bowls. With the short mat bowls the tendency is that none of them have ever played bowls before so we've taken the equipment there and we've demonstrated. Now after three or four years they phone us up and say we don't need you, we just want the equipment, which is great and a social group has developed from the inter-village competition. They meet, not necessarily to compete, or to train, they just meet socially, and that's what will be the by-product of this particular event that we organised.'

When the interview is over I mention casually that the only other person I know from Dyserth was my best man. 'My brother,' he says. It could have been a very different conversation.

Ronald Emlyn Davies, Rhyl, Clwyd

The Rhyl Labour Club at mid-day on a Friday. The majority of those sitting drinking or gathered around the snooker tables are over fifty, although families with young children occasionally enter. Ronnie Davies is obviously well-known. As he enters he is greeted from all sections of the large room and engages in brief conversations with friends on his way to meet me. He is seventy and a local borough councillor.

'I was born in Rhyl, in very close proximity to the Town Hall, number 49 Wellington Road. Son of William David Davies, M.M. and Gwladys Davies. My father won the M.M. in the 1914 War and met my mother in 1919. He was employed as a GPO engineer – pole erections in those days – wheeling poles as far as Denbigh from Rhyl on handcarts. He was actually born in Ynysybwl, south Wales. His father moved there when they were building the miners' houses and was employed by the coal owners and that's how he came to be born in south Wales, in Ynysybwl. A native of Denbigh, though. Now, I was one of five children, four boys and one girl. Three of us were educated, passed scholarships in those days, to go to the Rhyl County School, which I left at fifteen, because my mother's and father's wages weren't very high. Not enough to maintain a family of five – there were no child benefits then. Any road, I joined the LMS Railway – railwayman. Started in 1937, became a cleaner, eventually a footplateman, fireman, driver. Working out of Rhyl, Rhyl loco sheds. Happy times, very hard, hard work. Our wages as a fireman – top-grade fireman, mainline fireman – from Holyhead to Crewe were fifty shillings a week. A top-link driver was four pounds fifteen shillings a week. Eventually time took its toll, as it took its toll of a lot of locomotive sheds. It closed in 1963. Men had the opportunity of moving anywhere all over the country, but the wife – Welsh roots – no way was she leaving the area. Thorough Welsh, Welsh-speaking, Trelawnyd, a coalmining village in those days. All the men of the village were employed at Point of Ayr colliery.

'We reared a family of four. I got a job after the railway closed with a friend of mine who offered me employment as a bookmaker's clerk, until he sold the business to one of the conglomerates. And then I became manager of Rhyl Football Supporters' Club, licensed club.

'I've been a member of the Labour Party fifty-four years. In fact, my name is over the door here. And I've always been involved in politics, election campaigns . . . I remember 1945 very, very well. I had the pleasure of meeting Aneurin Bevan here, Clement Attlee. The old Pavilion here, which held nearly two thousand people was packed. Every meeting was packed during that election. Irene Lloyd-Jones, later became Irene White, was Member of Parliament for Flint North East. It was a wonderful campaign, 1945, and if there was an election today it would be exactly the same feeling. One of ecstasy to see a Labour Government returned.

'I joined the Council in 1974. Rhyl Urban District, Rhyl Town. In 1976 I was elected a Borough Councillor. I've seen the changes in Rhyl. Rhyl used to be a beautiful area. I remember doing a survey with the former town clerk of Rhyl, Mr Eric Fletcher, when we were asked to provide certain information for Government statistics in about 1977, '78. Rhyl was on the decline then and the question that was asked by the Welsh Office was, "What do you attribute the decline to?" And I've got it there in black and white. I said to the town clerk, "You put down in your reply that people have decided that long-term visitors are changing their habits. They're making their premises into flatlets." They eventually became all-year-round lets, because there was a shortage of housing for immigrants to the area from England. We noticed the change about 1980, that people were moving into the area, out of work. Unemployment had always been a problem in the area and they made it much worse. But accommodation became easy to get. People were out to make a quick buck, buying property that was quite low-priced. They were buying up large holiday residences and splitting them. And that's how it developed until we got the grants from the EEC to regenerate the area. The decline became so rapid, the unemployment figures were well in excess of the average . . . in one ward alone, the west ward, they were over forty-eight per cent. My ward was twenty-four per cent. But the Chief Executive Officer had a scheme, that the West End of Rhyl had become notorious and that it was time to do something about it, so applied to the EEC, Welsh Development Agency, Welsh Tourist Board, and we eventually got money to regenerate the West End of Rhyl. As you see it today it's not complete, but it's well on its way. All the houses have been renovated – in fact they're nearly brand new now – and houses in multiple occupation are very closely monitored now.

Rhyl in 1945, straight after the War . . . boom years. Everybody had money. They'd come in throngs. This place would be packed to the doors this time of year, packed. No longer. No longer. I suppose holiday habits have changed. Perhaps they'll stop two days now in Rhyl, three days. The car is available to them now and they don't stop for the fortnights like they used to. We had some wonderful hotels pre-War. We had a spa baths in one of the hotels – the Marine Hydro, known today as the Marina. All the top teams – Derby County, Aston Villa, Liverpool, Birmingham, Manchester City – all came to Rhyl. When the cup-ties started they used to come to do their training prior to the cup-ties. That sets the scene for what Rhyl was in those days. And it was a wonderful resort.

'I would envisage that in five years' time that we would be in the top bracket of holiday resorts in the country. Let us hope – I hope that I can see it – the harbour development, marina which there are plans for with moorings for about three hundred boats . . . We used to get boats here in pre-War days of a thousand, two thousand, three thousand tons with timber and cement. The river was a very good river then, but it's silted up now. No money was ever spent. Just like when you go into Cardiff and Newport now and you look at that, the derelict river mouth when the tide's out there. But that is the next scheme and I hope to see it.'

Mike Davison, Betws yn Rhos, Clwyd

Mike Davison first arrived in Wales in 1988 to renovate a cottage belonging to a member of his family and has lived here ever since. Formerly theatre manager with the Everyman in Liverpool, he is now editor of the Rhyl and Prestatyn Visitor, *working in a busy suite of offices up a flight of stairs in the centre of Rhyl. He has an extensive writing background, but his present post is his first experience of journalism.*

How did you learn your job?

'It's an absorption process, really. I suppose in a sense it's through people, through the very nature of the job. Just moving round the area you meet people, you learn a little more, you visit places, you learn something of the past history, the state of the community at the moment. And as a newspaper we're very much involved in all aspects of the community, the organisations, the official local government side of it and also the individual human stories that abound. They always say that behind every window there's a story . . . you pick up things faster than an ordinary citizen would because, I suppose, we're poking our noses into every corner of society for either good or bad reasons. The remit of the paper, obviously, is to tell the story of the community as well as selling as many papers as possible. We take a campaign – one notable one was the possible closure of the Point of Ayr colliery – and we very much backed the miners to keep the colliery open. Fortunately, touch wood, it is still operating, but its long-term future . . . well, that's anyone's guess. I feel that it will inevitably drop down, as it's doing at the moment, and may well end up in private hands or whatever, but either way our concern was for the miners, their families and the maintenance of the colliery as a working entity. To that end, over a long period of weeks, we followed the story, sort of spread it out into the human side, talking to miners, talking to their families and this sort of thing and giving it its own logo, its own identity, so that people could see over the weeks that it was a definite campaign, and we also supported with car stickers and posters and the rest of it. We now have a situation arising in Prestatyn, where there is a great possibility that the local community hospital will close. It's only a twelve-bed hospital, but it's very much a part of the town; it's a facility that's very much needed by the town and there's been a series of secret, behind-closed-doors meetings going on recently. Now we, again, would be very much behind any campaign, would support any campaign to keep that hospital open because we do feel that it is a needed facility.

'I think to a certain extent this job makes you less idealistic insomuch as you see – or you have to see – that there are two sides to every argument. There's always a practical side. It's all very well to say we want this wonderful environmental situation to go on here, for instance, but you have to look at other factors, you have to look at people's jobs, you have to look at financial or economic factors and all the rest of it which come into consideration. You know, you get very cynical. The cynical old hack, there's some truth in it. You get approached by every loony in creation, let's face it. Everybody's got a cause, whether it's that the council haven't painted their windows or they can't get a job or whatever – they all come knocking at our door. But as I said before, there are always two sides to every story, and you learn to detach yourself from it. I'm a bit like that anyway, but I think I've learned since I've been down here. When I first came down to live in the Clwyd hills, in a very, very rural situation, right up on top of a hill, it was "Oh you don't want to go down there, they hate the English", all this sort of business, which is a nonsense. Shall we say, there is a barrier against the arrogant English, who want to come into Wales, take it over, will not accept the needs, the history, the culture of the local community. But that is not significant of Wales itself, that is the same in any community. You go and live in Bradford and tell them they're all wrong and there was never a decent cricketer came out of Bradford: you'll get the same opposition. I personally have found the Welsh people to be particularly friendly, to accept me for what I am. Unfortunately, I have to admit, I haven't attempted to speak Welsh. I'm now married to somebody who was brought up speaking Welsh, who moved away and has since lost a lot of it, but is getting it back again. But I felt that at my age, with my rapidly reducing brain cells, I hadn't got the time, and to a certain extent the inclination, to go into formal lessons and try and take on the language. I felt it was too much.

Has that ever been a disadvantage?

'It's a disadvantage to anybody in north Wales in terms of career. There are certain areas where it's not necessary, but you apply for any job in a public area with some of the large firms in north Wales and if you're not a Welsh speaker you are immediately at a disadvantage. That hasn't directly affected me, but I can see that if I ever wanted to move on in north Wales, in terms of career, it could be a problem. But it's a problem I'm prepared to accept. I must say, though, that I'm fully behind any attempts in Wales to promote the language. What I will not support is the extremists. There is a way to do this and there is a way that the language will be kept and will continue. I don't think that the Welsh language is in danger of dying. I think that there is probably more interest in it now that there has been for a couple of generations and I think it will continue to thrive. But the answer is not in the extremists who want everything on this side of the Welsh border to be conducted in Welsh, that is not the way to do it. That is as arrogant as the English who come in and insist on everything being English. The way to do it is gradual, it's softly, softly; there is an interest, so promote that interest, let's keep it going. And the same goes for all Welsh culture.'

Frank Elliott, Johnston, Haverfordwest, Dyfed

Frank Elliott is a retired headteacher and a self-confessed eccentric. Born in Derby in 1944 to non-Welsh speaking parents from Swansea he was educated in the East Midlands and later taught there and in Kent. It became 'a family ambition' to return to Wales, and this he achieved in 1981, teaching first in Gwent and then in South Pembrokeshire.

'I was particularly anxious that my own children should have the opportunity to grow up here and then choose for themselves whether they had dual nationality or be English or Welsh. Now, it's been a great pleasure to me – more than a pleasure really, a homecoming – that gradually my children have shown an interest in Wales and Welsh. My twenty-five year-old daughter, who works for the civil service in Cardiff, is learning Welsh and my twenty year-old son was sat next to me, cheek by jowl, as we learned Welsh in Fishguard during last winter. That's been the cause of enormous satisfaction. Learning Welsh has given me an insight into the way my father spoke English. He spoke with a Swansea patois, very, very strongly influenced in his syntax by the Welsh language. And more than that, I feel that it stretches beyond my father . . . that I've actually shaken hands, in a way, with my grandfather and his family, who were native Welsh speakers. It means a great deal to me.

'Personally I feel very strongly that there is a Celtic identity. I think that I'm not politically correct and a good member of our society at the moment, because I think there's a lot of hocus pocus talked about issues like this multiculturalism nonsense. I mean, you can have a bowl of fruit, but an apple doesn't become a pear. As far as I'm concerned, I'm a very positive racist. I haven't got negative feelings about other races, in fact I respect them greatly, but I do feel that a race is a race, and whether one is a Jew or . . . an Afghan, or a Celt, then one should recognise that within oneself and look for the benefits that one can offer one's neighbours. In exactly the same as we can from our other gifts, whether we're musical or whether we're tall or whether we're strong. I personally happen to have some ability in mathematics, and that's an opportunity to share my talents with my neighbours. I think that we should be more . . . positive about our identities and our race.'

What about the current state of Welsh identity?

'We've been left with a curious inferiority complex in Wales. People always apologise for their Welsh and are shy to speak Welsh to a learner because they feel that it's not good enough. You don't get a Yorkshireman saying that he won't speak English because his English isn't good enough, or a Devonian saying something like that. It's just this curious wrongfootedness that we seem to have in Wales, that we're shy of our own identity. And people tend to hide it away. That's one of the reasons, I feel, why Welsh has been on the retreat. I noticed recently on a holiday in Ireland that the Irish seem to be much more positive, confident about their Irishness. They seemed more demonstrative than we are in their hospitality. Their hospitality remains hospitality and they don't change their ways for the visitors, whereas it seems to be a freak of nature in Wales that wherever you go it's the immigrants that are running things. The school PTA or the local council, even the local rugby club to a certain extent: it's got a Cockney as a president. There seems to be this shyness and inferiority complex in our Welshness. We're not assertive. And if you talk to another Welshman, we all seem to have been brought up to be offered the biscuit three times before you dare take it. Sometimes it annoys English visitors that when they're offered something – "Would you like a cup of tea?" – and they say, "No thankyou", we follow the ritual, "Oh, yes, you will have a cup of tea", and they say, "No thankyou". And they really don't want one. Whereas we've always been taught to refuse at least twice before you accept anything.'

A hypothetical question. Given the choice between the Irish experience of self-government and the virtual elimination of the language, or a thriving language in a Wales answerable to Westminster, which would you choose?

'Self-government without a doubt. Because I think that the language has got to float on its own merits. There is no way you can artificially keep a language alive. And unfortunately the people responsible for Welsh, the mandarin class, have done so much damage. The mandarin class stand to gain from keeping Welsh obscure and aloof. And this is tied to the problem that when you speak to ordinary people they never think that their Welsh is good enough. It's partly because you've got these academics in Wales who talk down to ordinary folk. Which is curious really, because there's a tradition in Wales of equality. There's been this trick in the last couple of hundred years where the learned few in the citadels at Aberystwyth or Lampeter or wherever look down on the rest of us. And unless you're sort of fourth dan black belt in BBC Welsh you're not good enough to speak it. But there is a kickback against that now. And I think that the real future for Welsh lies in the fact that people in Cardiff will move house and pit their wits in various social manoeuvres to make sure that their children go to a Welsh-medium school. For the best possible of all reasons – that Welsh-medium schools are *better*. The quality of life is better. The success in all kinds of endeavours – music, the children's play, examination results – everything in Welsh-medium schools is better. If you look at these dreadful league tables that the Government have got, the Welsh-medium schools are outstanding in every county in Wales. Where, say, the average school in West Glamorgan is getting thirty-five per cent of pupils through five O Levels, the Welsh-medium schools are getting about sixty per cent, which is a massive difference.'

Dyfed has traditionally been very supportive of the language. Do you anticipate that policy will change after local government reorganisation?

'Pembrokeshire people are very, very suspicious of Welsh. And very self-conscious about the fact that they have family traditions of monoglot English speakers. Milford Haven, Pembroke, Tenby. And those people feel threatened by any Welsh policy. For example, at the recent Euro Elections I noticed that the Plaid Cymru candidate toured Milford Haven broadcasting in Welsh. I don't know whether the poor man realised it or not, but that probably ruined his chances. Because, although Plaid Cymru offers marvellous policies for Pembrokeshire people, unfortunately they don't articulate those policies in English. If you're going to carry people with you you've got to win them.'

Is Welsh self-government viable?

'The European context has dramatically changed the public perception of Plaid Cymru. And also the growing awareness of people who have bothered to cross the Irish Sea that the Independent Republic of Eire hasn't created a Potato Republic. Those people are thriving in spite of the fact of being deprived of the benefit of Whitehall mandarins.'

Is Wales ready then?

'We've got a frightening legacy of corrupt socialist government at a local level in Wales. Now, I'm not against socialism *per se*, but I'm against the kind of corrupt socialist government that we've got in a lot of the Welsh counties. I worked in Gwent for a couple of years. It was like working in a Socialist Soviet Republic. The people are frightened to speak to you. There's a sense of an all-powerful, autocratic regime of Labour County Councillors who have got enormous power and wield it ruthlessly. You've near enough got to touch your cap to the local commissar. That's what worries me, can we survive that? I'm certain we could manage without London. Economically, there's plenty of wealth in Wales. You go across and look at Ireland and you see a better standard of living. Go across and look at Brittany, the same. And the reason is that they're not supporting London. London is a very, very expensive hobby.'

Will Wales be a better or worse place in ten, twenty years' time?

'I think that the whole of Britain has reached almost the point of disorder, the point of anarchy, with our democratic system being strained to its limits by the law and order issue. Swansea I love very dearly. I don't go there any more. It's not safe to park your car there – Cardiff's okay, funnily enough – but it's not safe to park a decent car in Swansea. If I do go, I make sure I park the car where I can see it. We meet a lot of holiday-makers in Pembrokeshire. And whenever I meet anyone I test them out about how they feel. We've got some people staying here at the moment from Caerffili. They're frightened to walk down the main street there at eleven o'clock at night. These are not old people. These are people about the same age as me. Now, whether the silent majority are going to start demanding real policing and real discipline, or whether we're going to fall into disorder . . . I mean, history tells us that this kind of situation is ripe for extremists. These are the situations where the Hitlers and the Stalins take over. The National Front are absolutely delighted every time these kinds of things happen.'

And the future of Welshness?

'I've talked about my Celtic inheritance. I think that in my own family case it's shared with very deep and sincere Christian traditions. It's affected my view about the continuance of the Welsh language. There were times when it really, really worried me and I thought I ought to rush out and do something. Then suddenly I realised with a blinding flash of clarity that – I don't like talking in these terms, but in very simple terms – that if God is with us then the language will thrive. If it's not the pattern, if it's not desirable, then the language will die, no matter what my sentimentality about it. It's no good wishing. There's got to be a natural sequence, an overview of how these things go. But not necessarily like these people who believe in global warming or all the other . . . trendy issues. The pattern is not necessarily dictated by the last fortnight. For example, I remember when I first started teaching in Bromley in Kent, we had to cane boys who had long hair. If their hair touched their collar they had to be caned. When I asked the older teachers why this was the case they said it was because it was tradition in Britain and good for boys to have short hair. So I pointed out that Clive of India and Captain Henry Morgan, Horatio Nelson and a lot of the great men who were revered who had made our Empire glorious, their hair was long, and in fact it was the short-haired prats that had lost the Empire. Now, they just couldn't see beyond the immediate pattern and they got very angry with me for pointing it out.'

Frank Elliott asks to close the interview with a story.

'During my father's life he did many beautiful things. One of the most beautiful was that he travelled to work in Derby – a three-mile bike ride – and unbeknown to any of us he scattered lupin seeds along the canal bank. And then one day when I was a young man and I was jogging and he was cycling he said to me, "What do you think of the lupins along here?" And I said, "They're absolutely fabulous, aren't they? Where do you think they came from?" "I know where they came from," he said. "I planted them." And it's always struck me in my memory of my father that it was a very . . . a very *Welsh* thing to do.'

John FitzGerald, Aberystwyth, Dyfed*

I recognise Father FitzGerald, Catholic chaplain at University College, Aberystwyth, from an interview he gave on television the previous evening. He is tall, genial and speaks immaculate Welsh. He was born sixty-seven years ago in Ludlow to Irish parents with roots in County Kerry. We settle to talk over tea at the Church in Wales tent on the field at the Eisteddfod.

'In January 1940 I came to Castell Brychan, a little Catholic school in Aberystwyth and it was there that I began to learn Welsh with John Saunders Lewis [*the critic and dramatist and one-time president of Plaid Cymru*] as my teacher. I left in 1942 and joined the Carmelites. That meant at the time that I had to go to Ireland and it was there that I joined the order and studied at University College Dublin. I was there for five years, studied theology with the Jesuits in Town Park in Dublin, then a year in Rome, three years in Cambridge and then back to Llandeilo to teach for two years in a residential school we had there. The school moved to Cheltenham and I stayed in Llandeilo where I spent a further six years teaching philosophy to members of the Carmelite order. I returned to Aberystwyth in 1954 as chaplain. I did that for six years and worked in the Philosophy Department in the College from 1970 until the Department disappeared from under us or over our heads and I was the last fig to fall from the tree last year. Now I'm back as chaplain again.

'Academic work has taken up most of my life, but I've got one foot in the parish as it were. There are three of us in the Aberystwyth parish and I'm one of the three, but with special responsibility for the students. The main thing about a university chaplain is . . . to be *available* and that means being known to the students as best you can so that they know – well, I hope they know – that you're a person they can turn to and in any event a friend. As things have turned out, coming back to the post of chaplain this time, having taught in the College, there's an advantage in the sense that I've got former students still in College who know me anyway, not that they're Catholics, most of them. There's that . . . and knowing the staff too, you know, so you're not working in a place which is unfamiliar to you. When I first came I knew very few, but this time I know lots. As I was saying, being available means putting yourself – without pushiness – putting yourself in view as it were. That means being ready to take part in debates *et cetera*, and of course you get invited to take part in certain kinds of debates. They think at once, they're talking about abortion, they think, "Oh, what about John?" And there was one last year, "This house is here to be queer". And I was asked – fair play to them, the students know me – they asked me to speak for abstention. And so I made a speech proposing an amendment, namely "This house is here to be human". And the president of the gays and lesbians in College, well he spoke from the floor to support my amendment. That's just a little example where you . . . seize an opportunity.

'A big difference between the end of the sixties and now is that students are less eager to sit down and discuss things seriously. I'm not talking about inside classes, now . . . When I was a student, and dealing with students after that, one of the things that people did was to discuss the problems of life and the world and so on into the depths of the night. But I've seen very little of that thus far. I'm afraid that for Thatcher's children, with all respect to them, even if they have a different political opinion, that a career and a degree are more important. There's another thing that must be said out of sympathy for them: they're under financial pressure, a lot of them. That means that they work in a chip shop or some other shop even during term time. They have to and that restricts their spare time. I'm not complaining about that; however the model I have from working as a chaplain previously meant including . . . saying, "Right, we'll have a discussion group'" and let anyone who wished to come do so. I remember something like that going on with twenty people for a term and then maybe just a handful would come the following term, but that's fine, you see. Well there we are, a chaplain's work is varied. It can be quiet at times too (!)

You learned Welsh at a time when there was no learners' 'industry' as such. How did people react to you in the forties?

'In the forties, with Saunders, what we learned in lessons was *iaith llyfr* – literary language. He had no particular method, or rather followed whatever method was available: Stephen J Williams's *Beginner's Welsh* and *Cystrawen yr Iaith Gymraeg* I remember in the second and third years. He'd come into the classroom and shoot sentences at us for us to translate as examples of a syntactical pattern or whatever . . . and reading poetry together. And so we had book language and I remember going down into town and going to shops. Well I could put a sentence together but I couldn't understand for the life of me what the girl – from the depths of Cardiganshire – answered back. I have an acquaintance *now* who speaks like that and needs to hear the same sentence twice if you shoot something unexpected at him . . . I think despite that that book language is a *solid* foundation. I went over to Ireland and after a year's novitiate in the order I was then in the college in Dublin and again had Welsh with John Lloyd-Jones who was a professor there and John Lloyd-Jones was used to teaching people following courses in Celtic Studies whose chief interest was in Irish. And so he started with some ancient book – *A Guide to Welsh* by someone, I don't remember who – and he started the first lesson by explaining the definite article. Not only explaining the definite article but explaining the *source* of the definite article and *comparing* the definite article in Welsh with the definite article in Irish and the definite article in Breton! And I was extremely pleased that I knew the two and a half years' Welsh that I had. But fair play to him, he was working in his own way . . . he lectured in English but he had to because it was that sort of class. By the end of the first year he said to me, "Well, I can't set a paper that's suitable for you because you're ahead of the others", and so there we are, I got a first class at the end of the first year! John Lloyd-Jones suggested that I should do Classics, so I did Classics after that and, fair play to him, that was a time when a professor's concern was for his students rather than for his department. After a year away from learning

Welsh officially I set to the following summer. I had John Morris-Jones's *Syntax*, Melville Richards's *Cystrawen y Frawddeg*, R T Jenkins's *Ffrainc a'i Phobl* and that was it and I sat down and worked my way through, comparing the syntax myself, reading R T Jenkins. If I couldn't say why he'd said such and such a thing I'd note it. If I came across a phrase that I wouldn't have thought of using for myself, I'd note it. What I was doing was applying to Welsh the method I'd learned doing Latin and Greek. You've got to master the thing, there's nobody else going to do it for you. And from then on it started to come.

'But of course you realise that you have to speak naturally and not like a book. My brother had done a degree in Welsh and French in Dublin and we'd read novels by Daniel Owen and Rowland Hughes, and by seeing the spoken language imitated in these novels we had some idea. When I came over from Ireland – I didn't travel often to see the family because it was war time but my father was ill and I travelled on the boat from Dun Laoghaire to Holyhead a couple of times. I had the idea of speaking to the sailors on the boat, the only time I was going to have a chance to speak Welsh. I remember one splendid evening: I was passed on from one sailor to the next, including one chap who I'm *sure* was a chapel deacon or something because his Welsh was rich. He didn't treat me like a teacher with a pupil, but he was very careful about what went on. After going to Cambridge the Mabinogion Society was running at the time and I saw a notice for a *noson lawen* and there I got to know more Welsh people in Cambridge and London University than I knew in Wales. And then, after I went to Llandeilo, I used the same method: right, I want to speak a comparatively local language. How to do that? In the first place read books by authors from the same county, take notice of the dialogue they use: Llywelyn Williams and D.J. Williams chiefly. And then the next thing was to go down to the shop on the square in Ffairfach and listen . . . and every time you heard something it was like collecting butterflies – Ah, they say that, do they? – and imitate. And the achievement was if you could say something, having put together a sentence based on a principle, and have people accept it as a natural sentence. And in Llandeilo I came on very well. I was there for eight years, and after coming to Aberystwyth and beginning to lecture to adults in the Extra Mural Department in Welsh that was excellent practice. I remember once saying to one class after one difficult lecture, "Well, I don't think that the class would have *taken* that lecture three years ago", and someone in the class said immediately, "And I don't believe that this lecturer would have *given* that lecture three years ago!" Well, there we are, I've had the opportunity and the honour to lecture in Welsh for getting on for a quarter of a century now. That means, very often, classes that are very often half Gog and half south Walian and that means that I say a mixture of *fo* and *fe*.'

We rise, say our goodbyes to the cluster of volunteers around the tea urn, and Father Fitzgerald, with a wave, ducks out into the sunlight.

Deborah Haigh-Roberts, Llandudno Junction, Gwynedd

Deborah Haigh-Roberts is seventeen. Born in Cambridgeshire, she was raised in Llandudno, her father's home town, from the age of six months. She is re-sitting her first year in the sixth form at Ysgol Aberconwy, taking A Levels in Music and French.

'I sing soprano. I want eventually to go to the Royal Northern College of Music to study singing because it does a course I want to do. I think it's a diploma – it's not a degree course and I've heard so much about it, and apparently everybody who goes there has the best chance of becoming a soloist. I've been singing for a year now and I'm currently doing Grade 4. Earlier this year an application form came through school – by chance really, they'd never done it before – from the Welsh Amateur Music Federation. They were doing auditions for new members of the National Youth Choir. So I thought, well, I'll just go for it because auditioning is a good thing really. So I applied and about three months later I got a date for an audition and I went. They said they'd let me know in about three weeks and three days later (!) they said, "We'd like you to join. We're willing to offer you a place in the National Youth Choir." So I went down down to Cardiff, and there were wonderful singers, and then went for a second practice, again to Cardiff. Me and a friend did a course this summer and went to Coventry Cathedral, Ammanford and Tenby and Llandaff Cathedral with the National Youth Brass Band of Wales and since then I've been singing with Côr Aberconwy and we've done various concerts around Gwynedd and places like Chirk Castle and Bodelwyddan Castle.

'There's a six-year opera training that I'd *love* to do, but then again you have to be really good at singing. I don't think I could maintain a career just in Wales, but I wouldn't want to move out of Wales for anything.'

And what's Llandudno Junction like?

'Well, I suppose it's quite big . . . it's not really a city. Actually I'd call it a town. And when you come through there's children everywhere because they've got nothing to do. I don't know really, I think it's a dump actually. I'd prefer to have lived in Conwy. It's just that kids vandalise everywhere. Wherever you go, there's some child smashing a bottle or giving abuse to an elderly person. I'd love to move out of the Junction, out of the area really. The problem with the sixth form is, after you leave you won't meet many of your friends again unless you go, probably, to the local night club. I wouldn't like to leave my really close friends behind, especially the music side because there's so many friends in Côr Aberconwy and the music teacher and other teachers in school I'm friendly with. I wouldn't like to leave it really. Wales is a beautiful place – apart from Llandudno Junction (!) – it's all the fresh air really and the mountains and the hills. I just love to get out there.'

What's the mood at school at the moment? How hopeful are people about their careers?

'Well, they're all stressed out at the moment, they're doing their mock exams. Like, you know, "We're gonna fail, we're gonna fail," but I think some of them are going to get somewhere. A friend who I'm in the National Youth Choir with – James Roscoe – has got a choral scholarship to Cambridge and so if he gets the grades that he needs then he's off there. I've got friends who want to be barristers . . . physiotherapists and really they're just worried about their exams at the moment because they're just round the corner again. There's so much careers advice now. Everywhere you go it's like, "What are you going to do?" I'm in lower sixth and they've started to talk about careers now – like careers advice and things. The school's been really supportive. The music teacher's been really great, actually. He's put me in a great position to sing in various concerts. I always do a solo in whatever concert we do, whether it's in school or outside and I've had a few donations of money to go to the National Youth Choir because the course fee was £170. The PTA donated money. Some of my friends are a bit jealous . . . just a few, really

. . . but the others are really happy for me, and the teachers. A friend I had before, who left in the fifth form, had a great voice and I didn't have one then because it came when I turned sixteen – I just opened my mouth and . . . out came this voice.

'I don't really like modern music. I prefer to sing masses and really classical . . . and I love singing religious music. I quite like John Rutter, actually. He's contemporary and he's quite nice stuff, but I don't like pop music at all. I'll maybe sing a few hits, but I'll very, very rarely listen to the charts. I like Mozart's *Mass* and Vivaldi's *Mass* – that's really nice – and I *love* the *Messiah*. I know that inside out, I'm always listening to it.

'Next year, we're going to Brussels, Antwerp and Paris and then we're back in Wales for the Eisteddfod and then in September we have the tenth anniversary of the choir in St David's Hall, Cardiff. And in October there's a tele-recording of Fauré's *Requiem* with Bryn Terfel.'

How do you juggle this with working and A Levels?

'Well I've done re-sits this year. I should be in upper sixth this year, but I'm in the lower sixth because I worked so many days in the local chip shop. It's like Tuesday, Wednesday, Thursday and Friday, half-four till eight, and Saturday morning, Saturday night and I didn't have any time to work. When I got home it was just, "Oh, I'll leave homework till tomorrow and do it at school", but I never did it 'cos I was just so tired. I had problems with having to shift everything to do a concert and so I actually cut my hours down in work so . . . it's better now. I can do what I want really. Get my work done, go to concerts, sing in them and go and see others and do my school work at the same time.'

Ronnie Harries, Pontardawe, West Glamorgan*

Ronnie Harries is standing by a stall at the Eisteddfod. He was born in the Swansea Valley eighty-two years ago and moved back there after retiring in 1967.

'When I was born in Pontardawe, steel was everything. I wanted to get away, wanted to learn and London was the place. So I went to London. Mam wasn't happy, but I wanted to go on the stage, wanted to make films, wanted to go into the theatre. Well I went. It was tough. There was no money to be had. I remember going on the Swansea train with £2 in my pocket and when I reached London the next thing was, what's your interest, what sort of work do you want? Well, I remember seeing a chap with a stall at the end of the road and I asked him could I paint it? He thought I was off my head, you know. He asked me how much and I said £2. That was my first job in London and I got other odds and ends after that.

'Well, at the time I could dance and tap-dance and entertain. I met some people and they knew that I could speak Welsh and they said that Emlyn Williams was wanting to stage *The Corn is Green.* He came after me and said, "Listen now, you're not funny at all," he said. "You're a good actor, so act." And he said I could go on stage with him in *The Corn is Green.* This was around '36, '37. And the way it worked out was this. Somebody would fancy you. "Listen now, I've got a film, I want a Welsh character." John Hastings, people like that. I acted with people like Errol Flynn, Gene Kelly, Richard Attenborough. And the funny thing is this: the biggest people were the most modest. People like Flynn had been through the real world and they'd been kicked and taught and they were happy to say, "Right, I've done my bit and I'm humble." You'll find that with everyone who's really great, that they want to be kind to you. And I appeared in about fifty films, including *A Yank at Oxford* with Robert Taylor.

'But times were changing. Television was coming in. I went on the stage in London, I played the Palladium, Her Majesty's, the Dominion on Tottenham Court Road. Nothing used to come to you, you understand. You had to go after it. Nothing would come. You had to go after it. So if somebody found out in an audition that you couldn't do something you'd be out, so if they said, "Can you tap-dance?" you'd say, "Yes. Ta-daa, ta-daa, pa-tapa-dah." Or if somebody asked you what else you could do, you had to *do* it. But, like I said, television was coming in and that killed the stage. I went to Bradford, Leeds, the Glasgow Empire. But there was no respect. I remember Frankie Vaughan up in Glasgow and people throwing stuff at him during his act. I remember overhearing two people coming out of the theatre in Sunderland and one said about me, "That comedian was very good; I nearly laughed," he said. It toughened you. You became more familiar with yourself, more sure of yourself.

'I lost my wife in 1967 and that's when I came back. I write for television now. Plays and this and that and I still play the occasional part. Not that I'm worried about getting work, but it keeps your mind sharp, that's the point. And you meet people. "Nice to see you. Nice to see you." And I love to meet old friends, people I worked with years ago. And they say, "God, you're not still alive, are you?" I'm working on a play for television now: *Gwenno*. It's a little old lady living in some village. And I'll say this bit in English: *She's got clairvoyant psychic powers, but she doesn't know it.* And she says interesting things, and of course in the village they all think, "Strange woman". Some think she's a fortune-teller, but she's not really a fortune-teller. I hope all that makes some sense.'

At the end of our brief conversation, Ronnie Harries asks to borrow a piece of paper and a pen from me. He sits me on a stool, tilts my head, and, suddenly silent, begins to sketch me. In a few minutes he presents me with a profile portrait of myself. 'Here's to you, Robin,' *the message reads.* 'God bless'.

John Harrison, Monmouth, Gwent

John Harrison is the first face most people see when they arrive at the gates of Monmouth Boys' School, where he is head porter. He lives on site in a row of what were once almshouses. Originally from Liverpool, he travelled the world in the Merchant Navy from the age of fifteen and witnessed the atomic experiments on Christmas Island. We talk as we walk through the school's lawned courtyards and it is difficult to believe that the streets outside the walls are crowded with shoppers.

'The reason I am here is because I ended up at the silly age of fifty where I was too young to retire and too old to get a proper job as I call it. So I applied for this job here, and out of a hundred candidates I got the job. My working week is about sixty-seven hours basic; the job is varied – I meet everyone from the Pope to the pot man coming into the school. I have to be a postman, keyman, psychologist, wet nurse, father confessor, you name it, I'm it – and I enjoy the job immensely. I have five hundred and forty boys, forty-eight masters full-time and many peripatetic teachers whom I have to deal with. My other jobs include repairing fire extinguishers, damaged furniture – that sort of thing – but, primarily, once school is under way my job is there at the gate, oiling the wheels.

'In my real life, as I like to call it, I was an electrician, a maintenance engineer, but my factory down in South Wales – in Taffs Well there – closed down, and the very same week it closed down I smashed my leg up in a car accident and it took me two years to get back on my feet. By the time I did, any contacts I'd had for getting a new job or whatever had faded away. So I took a whole new tack. And also I'd had a lifetime of industry and I just didn't want the pressures any more. So here I am in Monmouth and enjoying every moment of it.

'The minute you come through that gate you're in a different world. It is, like any institution, institutionalised. We've got something like a hundred and fifty boarders here and the rest day-boys. The rules that apply in here would not necessarily apply outside. But providing you do your job here you've got a job for life, basically – it really is a wonderful set-up. And that goes for right across the board, from the Headmaster right down to the last person, i.e. me. The PE master, he's been here thirty-two years; the engineer who looks after the plant has been here all his working life; one of the art masters is an ex-Monmothian, came back and taught all his life here. The younger element, yes there's a quick turnover of them. They get something under their belt, you know, for the c.v. and move on. Others, they're ten, twelve, fifteen, twenty year established people. They're really good at what they do. To my mind, as a layman, they seem very tunnel-visioned. I always look at teachers and think that they've never been in the real world; they've come from school to uni to school, so very often whilst they're A1 at what they do, anything slightly aside they need help with and that's the sort of job I get conned for. The boys themselves: a mixed range of boys. When we're talking about five hundred boys obviously there are different characters – and you can see the winners as they come through the gate on day one, that in six or seven years' time they are going to be the boys going out with all the accolades and all the achievements. Others are just here because they're being paid for, basically. But if a boy has a talent – whether it be art, sport, whatever – it is brought out in here, in this school here; they will bring out the best in you and push you to a limit that you never thought you were capable of. It's the same across the board – sciences, sports, art, music, we've got a very good music set-up here. Last year we had three organ scholars; three out of one school is something. Our brass band have won gold this year up in Manchester at the nationals and you can't fault them. The rowers . . . I don't seem to know very much about the rowing teams; they're a very elitist lot, they tend to keep to themselves. And if anybody gets the accolades here, it's the rugby boys. So I know what's going on with the rugby boys, but I know boys from each section of the school and I've got these salient points I remember about a boy. I know perhaps about his parents here or his achievements there, and it's all part of my job.'

What incidents stand out in your mind since you came here?

'I had two little old ladies came in last year. They said they were trying to trace a relative, and I said, "Oh yes, what year were they here?" "1890." So I said, "Yes, come along to the archives." And I fished out the names of the two people they were looking for, and on the way to the library I said to them, "Did they achieve anything?" And she said, "No – one of them was expelled and the other one died of yellow fever." Well, I thought, why bother looking them up? But there we are, we found them. And at that time the fees were tremendous: £40 a year – and this was 1893. But we were able to track down, yes, the fees they paid, the years they'd been here, what they achieved through those years, and the ladies went on their way rejoicing – they'd found it.

'Another little incident. Over the back there is our gymnasium, swimming pool and what have you and the boiler house for the pool needs a chimney-stack. Now if you look at the chimney-stack it's very easy to mistake it for a minaret. And sure enough, some band of Asians were camping in a furniture van down on the park there, you see. So this next morning half a dozen of these guys turned up in their army blankets and beards and they obviously thought this was their minaret and the gym was their mosque and they were coming in to wash and to pray. I had to convince them otherwise. And these sorts of things happen all the time.

'It's very easy to get lost here in Monmouth in the narrow streets and there was this one morning I was standing there before assembly at the front of the gate and I could not convince these two little old ladies this was not the road to Chepstow because they'd driven into the school. So I was backing them out and the timber wagon was backing in. These sorts of things.'

A pair of youths pass through the car park, girlfriends in tow. They wave across and John waves back. 'See that one there? The tall one?' he says, almost proudly. 'Choral scholar and a rugby man. One of the nicest lads you could wish to meet.' A horn sounds as a Morris Minor crunches along the gravel drive.

Graham Hoyte, Presteigne, Powys

The sign on the post office in Presteigne informs you in Welsh that it is the first in Wales and in English that it is the last. Graham Hoyte is sheltering from the rain on the steps opposite with his Golden Retriever, a few bunches of sweet peas and a sign explaining that he is selling them in aid of the Multiple Sclerosis Society. He is seventy-one and managed tea estates in Ceylon/Sri Lanka from 1946 to 1957, and then worked in Britain, selling. He is now retired.

'I'm growing sweet peas in five different gardens . . . the owners let me, of course! I've only got room for a few plants in my own garden. I do the digging and grow the plants from seed. I put up the canes and the netting. I did it last year, and discovered that one owner had had multiple sclerosis for fifteen years. So, I thought it would be a good idea to give any money I earned from selling the sweet peas to the Multiple Sclerosis Society. We made £566.89 in 1993 and we've made £928.02 so far this year. I want to make £1000, but the sweet peas have a season – they "go over", as they say. We've had some very hot dry weather, and it's better to have moist weather like this, and they can keep going for weeks. I cut each row every day and a half – I find that's best. A real "cut-and-come-again" crop – a bit like plucking tea, really. Now I'm afraid we're coming to the end. A friend out at Kinsham has let me cut her sweet peas, and they must have raised over £120 for multiple sclerosis. After I'd been going for a fortnight this year, in the middle of July, I found a kind person in the town – a widow – to help me with the bunching. They're neatly done, aren't they? Big help, that – I couldn't manage without Muriel. I cut in the late afternoon and evenings, and take the loose flowers to Muriel for bunching – seven, eight, nine or ten blooms, according to the length of stems: twelve to fifteen for posies. That's my marketing, as all bunches are 50p apiece, and I've never had any grumbles. The sitting and selling is the worst part, though. I reckon only one in forty passers-by will stop to buy, and when you've got eighty or ninety bunches to sell in six or seven hours I get a bit naggy in myself! That isn't good, but I can't help my nature. It's worse when it's raining, but I come back here to the bit of shelter on these steps. No, we take no expenses. Anyone could make money for a charity, like this. It just takes time.'

What brought you to Presteigne?

'A friend from my Ceylon days lives here, and I visited him and his wife when I was married. We came down and I liked the look of the place, and when I divorced I decided I'd live here. I'm lucky in my neighbours. It's quiet, isn't it, it's gentle . . . I think everybody's well-behaved generally. If you roam around you'll find that it's got a quality of life and there's a lot of nice people live here I've found. I wouldn't say I've come to live here because it's *Wales* – it's just a happy accident. See, you're looking at England down there: that hill that's in the mist, that's all England. So I'm not wound up about it being Wales . . . I'm very fond of Wales as I am of England and Scotland and Ireland, I mean every place has got its charm hasn't it? I'm not a really strong nationalist and I don't like to see divisions among people. and I think the less we go on about our nationality . . . My father was English, my mother Scots, I was born in Swansea, I've got cousins in Belfast and I've got an auntie of a hundred and seven and a half there. My father's family have lived in England for hundreds of years, and my mother's in Scotland likewise. I've lived with different religions: on one estate in Ceylon there were four religions – Hindus, Buddhists, Muslims and Christians . . . four hundred and seventy-five acres of tea providing a living for nine hundred souls, and we all lived very peaceably with each other. We didn't try and convert each another to our particular religion, which I think is probably the happiest way to go on. As soon as you start persuading someone to worship your God instead of theirs, you're in trouble. Odd thing to say, seeing that two of my uncles were medical missionaries, and an aunt married a missionary.

'I found it easy to settle here. They're pleasant people . . . The big thing is, you've got a by-pass so all the heavy traffic goes past and the people who want to visit Presteigne can look around here quietly. I wish they would buy more. I think that I would like to make it almost compulsory – no, a moral obligation – that people . . . tourists who stop in little towns like ours shouldn't just lounge around, gawping, but would spend a bit of money on food, nick-nacks, antiques, whatever . . . flowers, even. Knighton is six miles over the hill that way and Kington is about the same this way. Both have large supermarkets, and Leominster – fourteen miles away – has four, so you have a lot of pressure to travel somewhere else to shop. Folk might save coppers on ordinary food, and then spend pounds on impulse buys – stuff they didn't really want, but are mesmerised into putting into their trolleys. Our three stores carry a super range of food and have everything we need to live – I treat them as my larder, and buy what I want, almost daily. They're open seven days a week, about fourteen hours a day. It's good value, and we've got two butchers and two fruit and veg shops – one of those stocks fresh fish – so we're really *damn* well off. But if we don't support these stores we could lose two or three in a year or two. I've come round to this way of thinking quite recently, because I can see what may happen, and realise that supermarkets are a bit of a con. So I am rather a convert, you could say. But I'm not changing my religion – we've got a good new rector coming soon! He can only be an improvement – but that's another story.

'I don't know where Presteigne's going to be in five, ten years' time. It depends how much we support ourselves, how loyal we are to our own community. Kayes, the die-casting foundry, is the biggest employer with about 220 workers – hard grafters all of them. And we've got some high-tech industries too, on the up-and-up, and a school which serves Knighton as well, with a Leisure Centre and swimming pool – we're really very, very lucky. But we residents *should* try to buy most of our needs here, or we'll dwindle away like some other places.

'We have a Festival for seven days at the end of August each year and I hope that that continues to be well attended. It attracts a lot of proficient people, but I think that a more forceful marketing scheme would get more bums on seats – after all it's the final ten or twenty per cent making a full house which really brings in the gravy. And this little town deserves to survive.'

Graham wrote about a month after the interview to say that he had since made £1748.29 from donations and the sale of sweet peas. His notebook records 2862 bunches sold in nine weeks.

Gwyn Siôn Ifan, Bala, Gwynedd*

Gwyn Siôn Ifan has been manager of Awen Meirion, the Welsh bookshop in the centre of Bala, for the past four years. He is employed by the shop's sixteen owners, a relatively common method of ownership at one time, but less so now.

'I worked in another shop in Mold for six and a half years up to 1990, a completely different shop, to be honest, completely different customers. Where I am here I'd say that eighty-five per cent of the customers are Welsh speakers and fifteen per cent from non-Welsh, tourists. Over in Mold it was the other way around – some twenty per cent Welsh-speaking, thirty per cent maybe, and the rest mostly non Welsh-speaking Welsh from Clwyd, English who'd come into Wales from Chester just over the border – it's very close there. The biggest difference I see is that I can make quite a good living from selling mostly books here although I also sell Welsh cards and cassettes. I'm not over-dependent on customers buying just English books. To tell the truth, sales of English books here are very low. I try to give the sort of things I sell a Celtic slant, but at present it's very difficult trying to find companies who sell books on, say, Brittany wholesale. Books on Ireland are quite easily available, on the country and on the language. Of course we've got very close ties here with the Irish because following the 1916 Easter Rising two thousand Irish prisoners were kept up in the village of Frongoch, about three miles out of the town. There's a very close connection around in that sense. Having said that you can make quite a good living, you've always got to go after extras like cassettes and a few crafts, T shirts and so on and provide some stuff for the tourist trade. That doesn't last long; the tourist season has shortened considerably from what it was, say ten, fifteen years ago.'

What about the state of the Welsh-language book trade?

'I'd say that what sells best here is books for children. Because of the shortage of novels in the past I think that adults have got used to not buying books. There's more provision now for the older age group – up to fourteen years old – than there was. There's a series called *Y Corryn* for the seven to nine age group and now you've got a new series, *Cled*, which is a very popular series – and the provision for that age group is quite full. Even so we could provide more original books in Welsh for the younger age range. There's not half enough original material, books where Welsh children can identify with the characters. Things for young people will sell here if there's a picture of a cow on it or a sheep or a tractor, you know. Those sorts of things are always popular. As for books of local interest, there haven't been many recently. There's one coming out November from *Gwasg Carreg Gwalch* on Robin Jac, from Llanuwchllyn who used to take part in the Isle of Man TT races – a nationalist and *englyn* writer. That should definitely be of local interest. But we certainly need something on the history of Bala and something on the history of Penllyn generally. There are too many presses in Wales putting out these weighty volumes on poetry. We want something light, historical. There's not that much . . . what we've had in the past is a book from a local author from Llanuwchllyn who published a book called *Drych Penllyn*, a book full of poetry and prose that had appeared at the beginning of this century in the local paper, the old *Seren*. That sold very well because, I'm pretty sure, it's the older generation who buy books. What's needed is something to attract the, say, fifteen to twenty-five generation. I don't know what anyone could publish, but certainly that age group don't buy books, unless of course they're for GCSE, A Level or university.'

Does winning a literary prize help sales of fiction?

'Definitely. Definitely. When you look at the Prose Medal winner, the *Gwobr Goffa Daniel Owen*, if there wasn't so much publicity given to that sort of book the sales, I'd think, would go down by half immediately. But because during Eisteddfod week someone gets publicity, gets attention, definitely there's an increase. You can see that on the Eisteddfod field.'

Meleri Wyn James, Llandeilo, Dyfed*

Meleri Wyn James, twenty-four, is deputy arts editor of the Lampeter-based Welsh-language weekly, Golwg, *launched in 1988. Born in Llandeilo and brought up in Aberporth, she has worked on the magazine since October 1993. We are speaking at the magazine's stand on the Eisteddfod field.*

'There are eight pages of arts coverage in *Golwg* each week and I'm responsible for commissioning work as regards creative writing and current affairs. I also write articles myself. There are ten of us altogether, four of us working on the editorial side. The circulation's around three thousand, but if you take into consideration that copies are passed around, then it's probably nearer ten.

'It's basically a current affairs magazine and one of the things we're trying to do is to do stories before anyone else so that we compete against other Welsh and English magazines like, for instance, the *Western Mail*. That's the big emphasis, that we do stories first, that we're up to the minute. I think there's perhaps been a tendency in the past few years to use more pictures and use bigger pictures rather than have a lot of text, and I think that that's generally true of English magazines too. I'd like to think that *Golwg* makes a contribution to the Welsh language because we try to keep the language quite *flexible* and appeal to young people, you know? There's a tendency in Wales to think that you've got the literary language and then the language people speak, but *Golwg* sort of tries to find a compromise between them. So perhaps we've made our language more flexible than it is in some of the other magazines, like *Barn*, *Taliesin* and suchlike. We try to get people who don't read Welsh books to read *Golwg* and with the arts pages perhaps people who don't buy *Barn*, or don't buy *Taliesin* will buy *Golwg*. We hope that we reach quite a big audience of young people because there's *Atolwg* every month and that's specially written to appeal to young people so I hope that there are more young people reading *Golwg* than other Welsh magazines. And we get a reaction. We get people on the phone saying "Oh, I like *Golwg*". . . or complaining sometimes.'

What's the current state of Welsh-language journalism?

'I'd say things are improving. Have you noticed how many different magazines are on sale at the moment? There are all sorts of things and that's great and I hope that the fact that *Golwg* exists has made some contribution to that, that people are saying, "Look at *Golwg*, it's bright, it's attractive." Since September 1993 we've had colour and that's made a difference, that you've got a coloured cover every week and coloured pages inside. That means that you can compete better with other magazines. You know, when somebody goes into a shop and they look at the row of magazines and they see something black and white and boring next to the English glossies, well perhaps they're not going to buy it, so that makes a difference. It's . . . a good thing to have competition, that you've things like *Ffrâl, Tu Chwith, Ffocws,* the film and television magazine. That's a brilliant thing. I hope *Golwg's* won its place by now and I think that seeing young people setting about producing magazines, that gives hope for the future. Who knows what we'll move on to next?'

Meleri is called across to meet someone. She smiles and is gone. I hover – then take out a subscription to the magazine.

Tony James, Pontypool, Gwent

The Job Club in Pontypool stands adjacent to the town's market. A notice on the door reminds clients that getting a job is a job in itself. Inside, people sit at rows of desks, perusing newspapers, writing application forms and using telephones. The walls are covered with Rolls of Honour for each month, listing the names of those who have found employment or places on training schemes. Tony James is fifty-three and visits the Club three times a week. Born in Talywaun, he left school at fifteen and worked as a warehouseman for Pilkington's in Pontypool for five years.

'I got fed up with that so I left and I went into hotels. I went to the Wellington Hotel in Brecon as a porter. I graduated then to bar staff, I was there about three or four years. After a time I began to be fed up, so I left and went home – and I decided to go then to the holiday camps. Butlin's had just opened in Barry Island in 1966. I had an interview, got the job, went there on the Friday. There wasn't a road put down, you was up to your eyes in muck, half the chalets wasn't finished. All the campers was coming in next day, which was about two hundred of them. There was about three hundred staff and two hundred campers, so the campers was outnumbered about two to one. Everything was all deserted, you know, all the bars – there was about three bars there, two ballrooms – everything, and hardly any campers in them. So the following weekend it went up a little bit more, a few more came in, and by then they'd managed to get the roads down and all the chalets finished.

'I worked there for the season and I went back home then for the Christmas week, which is the best time to go – Christmas, five days. And I did that for about three or four years. Anyway, I got fed up of that then so I thought I'd try Pontin's down Burnham on Sea, so I went down there and I stayed there working behind the bar for a couple of seasons like. Then, . . . well, I had a death in the family then, so I had to pack that in and come home to look after my dear father, like. When he passed away, then I . . . well I stayed on the dole more or less. There was no jobs about. I couldn't go away at that time because I was living on my own and when you're on a holiday camp you're there for about six months. So there you are. You can't leave a house empty for six months, not by here anyway.

'So I decided to join the Job Club. I came down and seen about it like. I've been here about two or three years, so I've had a few interviews for jobs *et cetera*, but no good. I decided then to go onto the scheme – Jobsearch, like, over at Trevethin. Just a handyman, pottering about. The pensioners have their lunch on a Monday which I could do . . . organise. I do a bit a bit of gardening there, I've painted it all out right from top to bottom. I still come here on the weekend.

'I've found this place very helpful. Great. I don't know what I'd have done without it. They're marvellous down here; nothing's too much trouble. If there's any query you want or anything like that, if they don't know they'll find out for you. So I'm still here like.'

Brinley Jenkins, Cardiff*

Brinley Jenkins is sixty-eight and a familiar face on Welsh language television, particularly for his role in the soap opera Pobol y Cwm. *At an early age he came under the influence of Richard Burton's own childhood mentor.*

'I was born in Port Talbot, educated at the Grammar School in Aberavon and my interest in drama started there, to be honest. Our English teacher was PH Burton and he produced plays each year and I got the opportunity to learn something about drama from him. He then became a producer with the BBC and I got the chance to take part in radio plays. But I went on from grammar school to training college and then became a teacher, in Luton, and from there into the navy and from the navy back to Luton and then Port Talbot, where I taught and became a part-time actor working with the BBC rep for some years. I then became a drama organiser in Breconshire and I was there for about fifteen years before taking up a drama lectureship in Cyncoed, Cardiff, and in Caerleon. I took early retirement in my mid fifties and I've been acting full-time ever since.

'In the very early days I didn't do much acting in Welsh. As I said, with PH Burton most of what I did was in English. But as time has gone on, more and more Welsh came in. I'd say that the most important part I've ever had was playing *Macbeth* on television, in the role of Macbeth for the BBC on stage at the Eisteddfod in Swansea in 1964. I had a lot of major roles at that time in Welsh: Creon in *Antigone* . . . and I've performed regularly in Welsh since then, and it's only recently that I've gone back to performing in English again. You see, ever since *Pobol y Cwm* I've been taking small television roles in English.

'As a Welsh actor, of course, you have the chance to perform in both languages and that's a help. In England, because there are more actors there's more competition – although there's plenty of competition in Wales, believe you me, and some excellent actors. But we have the opportunity to work in England and English actors don't have that opportunity in Wales, in Welsh at any rate.

'Because of the lack of full-time Welsh-language theatre companies I've been near enough restricted to television roles. The last time I was on stage was performing for *Theatr Cymru* in Bangor, playing a short touring run at the time of the Wrexham Eisteddfod in 1977.'

Do you feel equally at home performing in both languages?

'What I feel most at home with, of course, is the Welsh I speak naturally. I've got a part at the moment, a small part, in a series called *Licrys Orlsorts* and that's written in Swansea Valley dialect, that's my dialect you see. I feel completely at home with that . . . I think that I feel perhaps more at home, apart from performing in my own dialect, in English than I feel in Welsh, if it's written in some dialect from the North or whatever. I'm not so at home then, but when you work on it until you're fluent in it, it comes naturally to you then. But if you asked me to pick up a script and act, then I'd say either Swansea Valley Welsh, or English.'

Do you think that Welsh and English audiences perceive you differently?

'Well, the most obvious experience of that was performing in *Pobol y Cwm* because then you had the direct reaction of the Welsh-language audience. You'd go into a shop and they'd come up to you and recognise you as the character you played, and when you played the part you could see the people you were performing for. Apart from that, no. An audience is an audience.

'I had some trouble losing the character from *Pobol y Cwm*, but I've been fortunate, they give me whiskers and what have you and I've had plenty of work since then so I'm happy enough; I think he's gone by now. And I'm old enough, you know, and bald enough so that they can fix me up with wigs and the rest of it.'

As if from nowhere, Brinley Jenkins's wife is at his side. She looks used to this sort of intrusion.

Anna Vivian Jones, Swansea*

Born in 1961, Anna Vivian Jones lives in the very centre of Swansea and teaches at Ysgol Gyfun Gŵyr, a Welsh-medium comprehensive school.

'My origins, my grandparents on both sides, are working class: the pits and the steelworks. My parents were the first generation to receive a formal education and both of them went to university. My dad's a minister and Mam's a teacher – quite traditionally Welsh, you know (!) They were part of the first battle in the Swansea Valley to set up Welsh schools, so they were responsible in part for the two schools that I attended: Ysgol Gymraeg Pontardawe and Ysgol Gyfun Ystalyfera. So I was educated completely through the medium of Welsh and went on then to do modern languages, French and German at Bristol.

'It was a conscious decision at the time to leave Wales because I'd lived my life up until then so thoroughly in Welsh. . . It was my decision because I wanted the experience, something different. In spite of the tension over whether I should stay in Wales to do my degree, I finally decided that I wanted that different experience, knowing really that I'd always come back here to live. I lived abroad for a while – France for six months and Austria for three – and then after graduating I came back to Swansea to do teaching practice.'

What is your abiding memory of Bristol?

'Bristol University's a very middle class institution and I was the only Welsh speaker on the course and in the hostel where I lived, so I tended to be "the Welsh one" rather than Anna. People knew me because of my accent. I had trouble settling in because in a way I'd lived such a sheltered, Welsh life. In the Valley, you see, everybody knew me and knew my parents because my dad was a minister there. And then I found myself at a university that was extremely competitive academically and where the majority of the students had been to public schools and didn't even know that the Welsh language existed. And at the time I had – although I didn't realise it then, didn't know the term – what you could call a mild identity crisis, because these people were studying languages and knew about languages the world over and didn't know that Welsh existed. And I'd been living my life completely in Welsh just down the road as it were, down the M4. So it was hard. It would probably have been easier to have gone to a Welsh university and continued as part of a Welsh community. But I do feel that during that time I did . . . you know, in a way, do a lot of work for Wales. A lot of people learned about Wales through me. It surprised me how little people – in the University, that is – knew about my background and the language and the culture. They had no idea at all that it existed. So I do draw on that experience. I eventually regained the confidence that I'd almost lost during my first few years in Bristol – the sort of confidence that a strong sense of cultural identity should give. I think it gave me strength and also I think it does you good sometimes to see Wales from the outside.'

And you appreciated your Welshness more as a result?

'Definitely. It definitely strengthened my Welshness. I've seen both sides in a way, as a Welshwoman inside and outside Wales; and not just outside, but in a middle- to upper-class community which by its very nature looked down on Wales and thought it worthless. So, I came back to Swansea and did teaching practice and then I got the first post I applied for (!) and went up to Ysgol John Bright in Llandudno.

'Well, that was an interesting experience because I arrived there at a time of great tension. There were a lot of English people living in Llandudno, from Liverpool for instance, running businesses in seaside hotels, who were refusing to let their children learn Welsh at school. So there was tension over the language from the moment I arrived. Llandudno's a very Anglicised town and so after coming back to Wales I felt I was in the same atmosphere as before. It was odd, for example, having gone through four years of having people impersonating my accent, to have children in the North find it just as funny.

'I was only there two and a half years. Although the school staff were friendly, I didn't particularly like the town. You were living in an atmosphere where people were running Welshness down and refusing to embrace it at all. But I enjoyed it more when I moved over towards Bangor. I enjoyed that. It was a chance to get to know other places in Wales because it's very easy for people in the south not to take any interest in north Wales, so I'm pleased to have had the chance to live in a community up there. It's very different to down here. I've settled back into Swansea now.'

Was it homesickness that brought you back?

'No, not at all. Not homesickness. I just think there's more meaning to life in the south for me, especially around Swansea. It still surprises me how many people I was in school with have come back here to work. There seems to be an instinctive attraction drawing people back to this area. And our families are close, you know; we get on well together. Especially within Welsh circles, we all know one another, so it was the natural step to take to come back. My mam and dad have just come back from Minnesota after fifteen years away. It's been very exciting; it's been lovely.'

Anthony Jones, Llanelli, Dyfed

I had been informed that the Carmarthen Constituency Labour Party meet in a room over the hotel where we are staying. The meeting I patiently wait to finish is something rather different. Anthony Jones is thirty-nine, was born and bred in Llanelli and is a building contractor. For the past two seasons he has been Master of Fox Hounds with the Carmarthenshire hunt.

How did you first become interested in horses in a place like Llanelli?

'I don't know, I think it must have been hereditary somewhere because my father, despite being a town boy, had ridden horses as a youngster – never owned one, but he'd always ridden on the local farm or whatever was available and I did much the same. If I saw a horse I wanted to be with it and it got to the stage where, you know, it was a case of I was wasting too much time going everywhere else to ride horses that I had to get one for myself. I was about fourteen when I got my first pony. And of course my brother, who was a couple of years younger, he was interested as well. And after we'd proved to our parents that we *could* look after it and we *could* ride it, they got one then and it just escalated from there. I gave up horses for quite some time, actually, until my children were born and they developed an interest in horses, pushed by their father. We live on a farm now, so we've got our own land for the horses and everything else and we became involved with hunting at the invitation of the current master at the time some eight or nine years ago. You're not *necessarily* invited to join, you can just come along, but on this particular occasion, due to business contacts *et cetera*, we were invited to come out hunting with the Carmarthenshire hunt, which we did. We subsequently joined because we enjoyed it. Later on, when the Master at the time, Mr Trevor Jones, was due to retire, he asked me to join him as joint Master in his last season. During that season unfortunately he was taken very ill and had to retire, and I've continued this year, obviously by invitation of the Committee, as the sole Master.'

What are your duties as Master of Fox Hounds?

'I suppose my duties are to conduct hunting, look after and keep the pack of hounds, and obviously P.R. and good relations with farmers and landowners *etcetera*. Once we get out on to that hunting field, then it is my sole responsibility, whereas tonight at a Committee meeting, it is the Chairman of the Carmarthenshire Hunt who is in charge, if that's the right word. When we are on horseback or the hounds are present, then I am solely responsible for all activities.

'We ride to hounds twice a week, normally on a Tuesday and a Saturday. The season will start this year on the first Saturday in November and end on the last Saturday in February. Obviously we will hunt prior to that, but that's what they call Autumn hunting and that's generally done on foot.'

Is there much local opposition to the hunt?

'In this particular area, in Carmarthen, no, not a great deal. Our close neighbours, the Teifiside, the Vale of Clettwr, have in this last season seen some rather stiff opposition from antis and the like. But it's my opinion that they are ferried for a day out from the colleges in that area, Lampeter and Aberystwyth, purely to cause disruption and mayhem. But we here in Carmarthen are very, very lucky; we get very little disruption at all.'

How wide a field do you hunt over?

'Carmarthen hunts basically from Kidwelly in the east down as far as Pendine in the west. On the northward side up to Cynwyl Elfed, that's about as far as we go in that direction. Carmarthen's got quite a big country, it's neighboured by adjoining packs, Llandeilo, the Vale of Clettwr, and the Teifiside and the South Pembrokeshire right down on the coast. The local landowners and farmers are very accommodating. In all fairness, the farmers are making a living out of the land, they don't want to see twenty, thirty, forty horses tramping across the middle of fields on a wet winter's day, but when occasion arises and the land's fairly dry they are very helpful and will allow us to go. They will always allow the Master and the Huntsman to follow hounds anyway, but the general field, on occasions, has to stick to the roads at the very worst or stick to the hedgerows of the fields. We have around one hundred members, not all riding members. I would say we have about fifty-fifty riding members and people who follow in cars and farmer members . . . you have business people and you get young children coming out and their parents are ordinary working people. We've got quite a strong following of children. I can say, safely, ten under-twelves on a Saturday and two of my children are involved and ride to hounds every week.

'I think hunting in Wales is very strong. We celebrated our centenary some six years ago. I think wherever you go – especially the Valleys – I think it's very, very strong. In fact I think it's far more popular in the Valley areas than down here close to the coast. But certainly there's a very, very, very strong membership locally . . . South Pembs, one of the larger hunts in the area, I know they had a hunt ball not very long ago and they had something like twelve hundred people attending, so hunting is very, very strong here in Wales. Our membership is mainly locals; we have people who have moved down to this area from the Midlands. But mainly locals, definitely mainly Carmarthen people.'

Bob Jones, Taff's Well, Mid Glamorgan

Bob Jones is sixty-two and has lived in Taff's Well all his life. Since 1969 he has been a member of the Communist Party.

'The only time I left the village was when I was in the British Army. Prior to that I had been a miner at New Rockwood Colliery. Fifteen of us left the pit in 1955 and tried to join the navy. They told us we was too dull, so we got drunk and all went and joined the Welsh Regiment. When I joined the army I think people would claim I was a racist . . . to an extent a neofascist. But it was my experience in the British Army that converted me to my politics. It was my experiences that made me think what role we were playing in the British Army at that time. The situation was in Cyprus where I had two mates killed. And I come to ask the question, why was we fighting working-class people? Because we was never told the cause as such. When you're in the army you're brainwashed and you're always told just to listen to orders. The consequence of that was that I started to read. I was then posted to Germany. And in a library there, run by the YMCA, I picked up *Das Kapital*. It took me a long time to read it. I had to have a dictionary. And Marx's argument on Surplus Value convinced me.

'When I left the army I went back under ground. I was then working in Nantgarw. I used to take the *Morning Star* every day and argue politics in the night. I joined the Communist Party branch in Cardiff. I joined through anti-apartheid really. There was a demonstration there. I got talking to a few comrades and they invited me to join. Through the experience of working with comrades – political work, trade union work – I am what I am today.

'I think that the problem we've got now is that we're having no discussion in pubs – political discussion. We've lost our culture as such. The Valleys are a classic example, where you had choirs, dramatic societies, libraries . . . now, to go in the Rhondda Valley, it breaks my heart. You've got fascist graffiti on Maerdy Hall, which hasn't been wiped out. And what we're trying to do now is get political discussion going. We don't argue that our politics are correct ones. We would hope that people would sit down, discuss and debate with us . . . and hopefully we could work together to change society.

'At first it was hard for me to call somebody Comrade. Now I call everybody Comrade. Especially if I forget their names; it's either Butty or Comrade. I found it very hard to use that terminology. I think that one of the reasons was that the anti-Soviet propaganda had been banged into us over the years. To be known as a Communist, I think, was hard for me in the beginning. Because being ex-British Army and all that, I was sort of frightened of the power of people pointing you out when you went in a pub and there was this "Stalinist" or "Stalin's come in" or "Stalin's batman" when you were discussing politics. I've overcome that. I'm a great one to argue now. I starts the arguments going. I don't mind being called Comrade.'

The Communist Party is calling for 'A Parliament for the People of Wales'. What lies behind that?

'Historically, it was the Communist Party in the early twenties that called for a parliament for Wales and Scotland. It took us many years to win the battle of ideas outside Plaid Cymru. It took a long time to convince the Labour Party that we needed a parliament for Wales. We're calling not just for a talking shop but a parliament with tax-raising powers and we would argue the same for Scotland and the regions of England, where democracy, by devolving power, creates more democracy.'

Does that go hand-in-hand with independence?

'No. Personally I would argue – maybe others in the Party would take a different line – that we would have a parliament for Wales and also a parliament, or some sort of convention, on behalf of all of us in Britain. At the same time I would argue for a united Ireland. I don't think that that's a contradiction really. But a Protestant Irishman would argue differently.

'Wales would take a bit of time to re-build. The coal mining industry for example. It's tragic that that was destroyed. If we did have a parliament and decided that we would open up our coal fields, nobody can just go under ground and dig coal. There's many trades. People are given the image of a coal miner as someone with a pick and shovel who just bangs the coal out. But there's people who use computers, there's engineers, there's fitters. It embraces all trades.

'I think that in the near future there'll be a market for our coal. The tragedy is that most of the coal that's being imported into South Wales at the moment is coming from Third World countries. For example, Colombia, where eight year-olds are producing it. I think that it might take some time, but I can see within the next fifteen, sixteen years we'll need our coal again. The problem we will get is to have a workforce that's capable of producing that coal.'

Is the Welsh coal industry salvageable, then?

'Oh yes, definitely. There's more coal left at Maerdy and Tower than have been extracted from there. Where I live in Taff's Well there's Garth Mountain, the gateway to the Valley, there's twenty-six workable seams. Now, if the Japanese had it, we'd be playing bowls over there. That's my argument to people. It haven't been scratched. Nantgarw just took a little bit of it, like. And it's there to be exploited. You could create drift mines, but then there's the placing of them mines. Nantgarw's situated in the Valley and we tunnel under the mountain. But with a drift mine, your waste would be tipped on the side of the mountain. Unless new technology comes in and you pack it underground.'

Is Wales economically strong enough to revitalize the coal industry?

'The best way I can put it is that we're being ripped off by taxation. I don't know the exact figure, but there's more money taken out of Wales in taxes and a very small percentage put back into Wales. The biggest share for the regions and Scotland was wasted on the arms bill. I never saw it as the Soviet Union being our enemy, but there was a ploy to con people that we needed a big defence, as they put it. I would argue that it was offensive, given my experience in the army. Malaya went on, Korea went on, all in my time. As a rule, in a war situation, they put the Scotch and the Welsh in first. I would argue the reason for that is, because in the regiment I was in, the catchment area would cover from Haverfordwest to Newport . . . running along the Breconshire border. Then from Brecon up to Wrexham, it was the South Wales Borderers. Then from Wrexham – the rest of North Wales – it was the Fusiliers. If in a war situation, for example, you get twenty-five killed, it could be one in Pembroke, one in Swansea, one in Taff's Well and spread round the Valleys. So people would say, "It's a pity Bob Jones has gone on" like. But if that happened to an English Regiment, where the catchment area was Liverpool, for example, it would be twenty-five lads from Liverpool, so people would question, "Why are our boys getting shot?" That's been the question in Ireland all these years, but it was always stifled.'

What sort of reception are Communist arguments receiving in Wales at present?

'Very good. Robert Griffiths, the Secretary of the Party, a Welsh-speaker, is a big advantage to us. In the last European elections we had two thousand votes. I know it's a big population, but two thousand votes. And out of that campaign twelve people have joined the Party. So, yes, I'm very optimistic.'

Brian Jones, Beaumaris, Gwynedd

It is festival week. Strings of fairy lights hang the length of the main street from the beach, up past the church, to the Sailors Return Inn. Brian Jones comes in with his wife, Ruth. They have been running the local post office for eight weeks. He is neat, balding and has a natural smile; a man clearly at home in a pub atmosphere. He speaks with a slight, yet unmistakable Merseyside accent. He was born in Liverpool in 1935, the son of an architect who ran a building firm. In 1940 the family were bombed out in the War and moved to the Wirral. Following secondary school in Birkenhead, he became apprenticed as a draughtsman, working back in Liverpool. At twenty-two, just before he was called up for National Service he married. He spent two successful years in the RAMC, was promoted to corporal within nine months and sergeant three months later. He left the Army in 1960 with a young son and went back to the firm where he'd worked previously, but couldn't settle to 'a grassroots job'.

'I went into engineering, working at Vauxhall Motors in Ellesmere Port and we bought our first house. It cost fifteen hundred pounds.'

'Thirteen hundred,' *Ruth corrects him.*

'Thirteen hundred. Four bedrooms, semi-detached, with a large piece of land at the side. After a couple of years or so we sold it and bought a very tumbledown housey-shop sort of place in Birkenhead. We opened a general stores selling everything from knickers to cooked meats and fruit and all the rest of it. My wife ran that and I carried on in engineering . . . we were there eight years. Eventually we sold the shop and moved out to a place called Greasby and we lived there sixteen years. I fancied a change, so I left Vauxhall and started working for Hickson's Brewery in Liverpool as a trainee manager. I worked for fifteen, sixteen, seventeen months in a pub in New Brighton. Then a chap from the brewery came in one day and asked me if we wanted a pub of our own. I said that that was the general idea, but that we'd had no offers.

'Anyway. . . he knew someone who was looking for a manager for a very busy youngsters' pub in New Brighton. We worked there for two years, did very, very well, but in the meantime we'd decided that we wanted our own pub. Tetley Walker wanted someone for the Mermaid near the station in Rhyl, so that was it.'

'We moved to Wales in 1983. We very much thought that we were now moving to Wales and that everything was going to be Welsh so I went into Marks and Spencers and bought a red sweater with a big dragon on it. Well, the Mermaid turned out to be occupied by drunken Irishmen, a lot of Liverpool, a lot of Manchester . . . the occasional Welshman used to come in, just to see how we lived, I think. We were there for nearly two years and, basically, we decided that we couldn't have a fight every night, we were getting brassed off with this. Well, they said, you've done very well here, we've got a pub in a place called Glan Conway, about a mile from Conway Castle. We'd had some marvellous times in Rhyl, but really . . . Are you Irish, or have you got any connections with Ireland? Well, they *love* a good fight. They don't mean anything by it. I'll smack you on the head and you'll hit me on the head with a shovel, and the next day we're best of buddies sort of thing. They call it the crack, and they genuinely seem to enjoy it. There were some baddies in Rhyl, but they weren't anywhere near as rough as we found them on Merseyside.

'Anyway . . . we went to Glan Conway and we were there for seven, no, eight years. We bought a house there. Then three years ago we decided that we'd had enough of pubs. You don't finish work until about eleven, half eleven, seven days a week and we needed a little break . . . Well, my wife's got two older brothers and a sister in Australia, so eighteen months ago we went out to visit them and we stayed out there for four months. In the meantime we were hatching this plan about what we could do to support ourselves. My wife had this idea of a post office. When we came back we approached various people and we started the process of getting a little post office somewhere. We were accepted and got this one in Beaumaris. We settled on the price, but it took six months between then and moving in.

'In the meantime we ran a little pub called the "Pen y Cefn" in Llandegfan, just up the road. When we moved there we got a slight shock because the language is very strong. We'd come across a little bit of Welsh in Rhyl, and in Glan Conway the old people speak it, but in Llandegfan *everybody* seems to. It's like a little world on its own. Well, we don't speak it, just little bits, but they took to us. When we were leaving they had banners round the pub and going-away presents and bouquets of flowers. It was crazy. We had no connection with them. It was wonderful, really. If you saw this place when it was empty you wouldn't think twice about it . . it isn't scruffy, but it hasn't got any particular atmosphere. But the people made us so welcome. We've got a friend in business in Caernarfon and when we went to Anglesey, he said that we wouldn't like the people. He'd lived here at some time and said they were a horrible lot, but we never found that at all. Banners all round the pub. "Best of Luck for the Future." Wonderful.

'I don't think that anything would induce us to go back to Merseyside now and I suppose that our plan is to retire here. We've got four children – three are married – and we've got ten grandchildren. They don't need us, really . . .

'Anglesey is very mellow. Working in a post office we get both ends of the spectrum: mothers with their milk tokens and old people with their pensions. Beaumaris is more anglicised, a town that is more like an overgrown village to me. You can walk around it in about ten or fifteen minutes. It's got everything you need, really. It's fine unless you want a disco or something.

'Although I'm Jones, I've got no real connection with Wales. My mum was Manx, and my dad was Liverpool, so I don't know what that makes me. My uncle had a pub somewhere in Wales years and years ago and we used to come to Wales on holiday when we were kids. Caernarfon. That was a wowie. That was a long trip. It took about three and a half hours in the car.'

Emyr Jones, Llanrwst, Gwynedd*

Emyr Jones is a native of Chwilog, Eifionydd. He was educated at Pwllheli Grammar School and Trinity College, Carmarthen He taught for one year in Aberdare before deciding on a career in journalism. In this capacity he worked on the Merthyr Express, Wrexham Leader *and as a freelance, contributing to local and national newspapers and television news. Having decided to return to north Wales, he worked for a time in a pub kept by his sister and brother in law in Arfon. In order to remain in north Wales he joined the civil service in 1979, working primarily in the Jobcentre Service, for the past twelve years in Bangor. He has been involved in editing the local community newspaper, or* papur bro, Y Pentan *for fifteen years.*

His wife teaches Welsh and his two daughters are studying Welsh at university.

'It's because I had some sort of journalistic experience that I became involved. I went along to a meeting about setting up a *papur bro* for Penmaenmawr, Llanfairfechan, Llandudno, Conwy and Dyffryn Conwy as far down as Llanrwst and I wasn't expecting to get a job, but I accepted it anyway, as co-editor as it was then. It's too big an area, to be honest. There's no natural connection – nothing that's common – between the different parts. It's too widespread. And that poses problems . . . has posed problems from the outset. Because one is conscious that the Conwy, Penmaenmawr, Llanfairfechan area just couldn't sustain a *papur bro,* it would be unfair to leave them out. The way I think about a *papur bro* is as an area talking to itself, and the more compact the area is the more successful it should be. You've got to have an area that fits together naturally. Our circulation at first was around fifteen hundred if I remember rightly. It has gone down, and the main reason for that is shortage of volunteers. We had distributors to start with, people who were willing to take an armful of copies around the streets in their own neighbourhoods and knock on doors. That's all stopped and as a result circulation's gone down to around twelve hundred. It's very difficult to get contributors, it's very difficult to get people to help put the paper together. *Two of us* have been compiling it for the last three issues, and it's unreasonable to expect two people to compile an eighteen- or twenty-page paper, or however many pages it might be. There are plenty of educated people in the area, but persuading them to put a few words on paper is terrifically difficult. There are crowds of teachers who've taken early retirement, headteachers who've taken early retirement, but despite all appeals they don't offer their services.

'I worry about the paper's future. I've been editor for fifteen years and it's far too long, more from the paper's point of view than mine personally. You need someone with new ideas, with a different set of acquaintances and friends to the ones I have, to draw on and encourage to make a contribution. I've bled every acquaintance I have dry by now, I think. Some *papurau bro* have found themselves in the fortunate position of being able to have a different editor for each issue over the course of a year. That lightens the load terrifically. I've not been able to do that. I can't get anyone to take responsibility for even one issue, never mind twelve. I suppose it means there's continuity, but after fifteen years you can have too much continuity.'

What's your editorial policy?

'I try to keep the paper apolitical, and the main reason for that is that the *papur bro* is the only Welsh that the majority of readers read. If you were to become political – for any party, now – there's a danger that we'd lose a proportion of the readership. And the result would be that they probably wouldn't read a word of Welsh. It also gives people a chance to write in Welsh. There are people, I'm sure, when the paper started who hadn't written a word of Welsh for years. One of the great pleasures is seeing – if we have contributors from the different villages and so on – how there's less correction to do as they become more fluent, more used to writing in Welsh. But I do feel that the popularity of *papurau bro* has passed its peak. For whatever reason, I think there's been a decline within communities and everywhere else, and it all seems to be happening together. It's hard to get people to join societies, whether it's the literary society or whatever sort of society. People just don't turn out. They distance themselves . . . keep to their houses and their televisions or whatever. And making a contribution to society has definitely gone down, which means that it's much harder for someone like me who's still struggling on. We've had meetings of *papur bro* editors from time to time and the complaints are more or less common to the rest of the *papurau bro*: lack of support. Some papers have financial problems, but we're fortunate in that respect. One of the extra things we've managed to do is set up an annual drama festival. There were two ideas behind it to tell the truth. One was to make a profit, and be an aid to support the paper, and the second was that there had been a tradition of drama companies in a number of the villages in Dyffryn Conwy. That tradition had stopped, and so it was our intention to revitalise that enthusiasm for drama and get people to re-establish village companies. It worked for some years, but we're finding it harder now to put on a festival of a decent standard in Conwy each year. The festival's very much appreciated and enjoyed and the hall's almost always full apart from those evenings when there's something else on locally.

'Financially, we're very secure. Each issue costs somewhere between seven and eight hundred a month, so we can't ignore the financial side. We try to be as professional as we can, take care that we've got enough advertisers, that people pay to advertise, so that we don't get into debt with anyone or in danger of failing because we don't have the cash. But the future? I don't know, to tell you the truth. Unless help comes I don't feel that I can continue because of pressure of work and so on to support the cause with fewer and fewer people. I'm not too hopeful, to be honest, unless more people offer more help and realise how important a paper like this is to an area like Dyffryn Conwy.'

Over the fifteen years, does any story stand out in your memory?

'There's a man of Polish extraction living in Eglwysfach. He's been living there since the 'forties, married to a local girl. He came across a girl from Poland who was on holiday in the area and when they were speaking, he learned that she knew a cousin of his. He also learned that his own parents were still alive, aged ninety-two. He didn't know. He'd lost all contact with his family. Anyway, this girl put him in contact, said where they lived and so on. Unfortunately, his mother died, but about a month, six weeks ago, he went with his family to Poland to meet his father. So we've been carrying that story, with pictures of them in Poland, his children with their grandfather and so on. So I see it as having given the paper an international flavour if you like! And the media went after it too, after us.'

The whole papur bro *movement grew out of an enthusiasm for local news in Welsh. Is there something more than a sense of duty that makes readers buy* papurau bro *now?*

'Yes, I think so. Possibly force of habit has something to do with it too. I'm sure there'd be a gap if they suddenly stopped, if people suddenly realised, "This village isn't going to appear in print again." I'm sure they'd be missed. They've become more or less an institution. There's got to be enthusiasm, too, or nobody would be willing to take the work on and certainly it's a . . . a merciless situation. The stuff comes in every month and you can't just say, "I haven't got much patience with it this month." You've *got* to do it because it's there. So you set to and you start again from month to month and the thing goes on and on and on. You try to be as enthusiastic as you can, but the situation *does* tends to make you a bit cynical. The sadness in the whole thing is that there is this unwillingness in people, that they can't realise how important a *papur bro* is and that they don't consider it important enough to sit down and contribute to it. That's the great sadness – people, well-known people . . . For example we had the National Eisteddfod in Dyffryn Conwy in 1989. There were people coming out of holes everywhere because there was attention to be had. But, of course, this is work from month to month, for very little acknowledgement or attention, but that's much more important work than an Eisteddfod once in a while. Work that lasts for fifteen years is bound to be more important than an Eisteddfod that visits once every quarter of a century.

'I still see the function of a *papur bro* as a very positive one. Your enthusiasm for the survival of the language encourages you to stick with it and carry on the best you can.'

Within a week of our conversation I am sent a scrupulously edited transcript.

Jeanette Jones, Llandovery, Dyfed

Jeanette Jones is fifty-one. She and her husband, Tom, own the Belle Vue Dairy, delivering milk throughout the town and surrounding area three times a week. They also run a small grocery outlet from the same premises. Born in Glossop, she has spent almost all her adult life in Wales. We spoke in the living quarters attached to the shop.

'I moved to North Wales when I was twelve years old, so I can speak Welsh. I was educated at Ysgol Dyffryn Nantlle, Penygroes, then I went to the Normal College in Bangor to train to be a teacher and eventually went down to London. I met my husband, who is of Welsh origin, at the London Welsh Club and I taught at the Heathrow Airport school. My husband was in the transport business as a manager but he didn't like the rat race and we heard that this business in Wales was coming up for sale because it belonged to a second cousin of my husband's. From the business point of view, it was a very flourishing town when we first came. Local farmers always used to come down into the town and they always used to bring their wives, and their fathers and their mothers, and they all used to meet at the Castle and the King's Head and have a good chinwag. And you used to get people in their eighties and nineties coming down. This was before all the shops in the town started selling milk.

'The first big change came with the auctioneers changing the mart to a Saturday, because they already had a very big mart in St Clears on a Friday. That destroyed the whole social pattern of the town as far as I'm concerned, because it meant that on a Saturday the farmers couldn't go to the bank, they couldn't go to the solicitor. The children were at home, so when the farmers came in their wives stayed at home. They didn't come any more, so consequently we lost that trade. I belonged to the Tourist and Trader's Association, and they did what they could, but it was too late. This had been done prior to them getting knowledge of it. They couldn't persuade the auctioneers to change. A lot of our customers were farmers. The fact that I spoke Welsh helped because it was continuity with the previous owners. My Welsh was a little bit *Gog*, as it were, *chwithig* as we call it, or *lletchwith* [awkward] as they say down here.

'So that was one big thing. Then after that you got the growth of supermarket trade and the advent of the polybottle for milk. We couldn't compete on the same terms. We *had* a very big round and what's happening now is that people are having seven pints a week where they used to have double that, and making up the difference from the supermarkets. People are supermarket-orientated now. Doorstep deliveries have gone down completely, from about eighty per cent ten years ago to, I think, around fifty. We're the last bastions, if you like, of milk deliveries.'

Is it likely that the business will have to contract?

'In fact, I've been supply teaching and I'm hoping to take up a permanent part-time post at the local high school, teaching lower school geography. I enjoy teaching; I've always wanted to get back into teaching, and it does pay for the overheads and help to keep us running. We try to keep milk at a steady price, below market price in some areas.'

How easily did you settle to life in Llandovery?

'I don't think I've ever found it difficult settling anywhere because I'm that sort of person. I think, coming from Derbyshire, you tend to be very friendly. It's not that cold feeling that you get in the south where no one wants to know you. And I lived in north Wales, which again was very friendly, but a different type of friendliness. The north Walians are very resentful of English people, very resentful of any intrusion whatsoever. I mean, they're far keener than Dyfed as far as keeping the language going and so on goes. I prefer the south Walians and I would never ever like to move anywhere else . . . I find the Welsh down here is a softer Welsh, the people are far more hospitable towards foreigners. They consider me Welsh although I say I'm not, I'm one of the *Saeson*. But they say, "No, no, you're Welsh." I think the only thing I could never get into as far as the Welsh are concerned is the humour. You know, the sort of *Jac-y-Do* type humour. It doesn't appeal to me at all. What I thought was excellent, and I've seen it twice on television here and I've also seen it at school, was the film *Hedd Wyn*. And that depicted north Wales as I knew it, or around there, the Trawsfynydd area, and I could relate to that. But, funnily enough, the children here could not because they couldn't understand half the Welsh. I find that I can understand nearly everything that I read. I don't read very much, not unless I have too, because it takes so much concentration. I read the *Lloffwr*, we have the *Lloffwr* [community newspaper]. I usually read that from cover to cover simply to prove to myself that I can understand it all, and if there are any new words I usually look them up and try to memorise them. I can converse in Welsh reasonably well, depending on to whom I'm speaking . . . I find I can understand things in north Walian Welsh better. I've just been to a thirtieth reunion in Bangor – the first time in thirty years – and immediately I heard the Welsh I felt I was at home from the language point of view because I understood them and every word that was said. Because if you get the colloquial Welsh going round here and if people speak very quickly I just have to pick up the gist of it. '

How much Welsh do you use in your day-to-day life?

'Not very much. Not unless I had to. But I'm not shy speaking Welsh at all, no matter to whom. I've been to Llanddeusant and some of the other schools which are Welsh medium in the area, teaching the infants. One thing I don't agree with and that is trying to teach English children Welsh. Because I've taught in all the schools in the area I know that the ones who are just below average – and say they might be off ill and miss a little bit – can't cope with that. They are coming through school and they're not literate in either language. And unfortunately you're getting quite a large percentage of these kids coming through now who are having terrific difficulty . . . and I'm taking kiddies now for special English lessons, trying to teach them how to read English because they learned phonetically . . . and they use

Welsh phonetics. You think of words like *enough*, they can't visualize it, they can't sound it out or anything. I'm having to teach these kiddies the shape of those letters and say remember that shape, that's the sound that shape makes. Not to write English, because I don't think they'll ever be able to spell correctly, but read English so that they can get by. Because some of these are from farming communities, this particular boy that I'm dealing with at the moment is a Welsh lad, who's been brought up through the Welsh medium and he couldn't cope with transference at the age of seven to English as well because of lack of background and intelligence. It's very, very sad. The remedy is to allow these children to choose English or Welsh depending on their ability and the language will still remain rather than it being forced on these kiddies.'

Do you foresee any changes when Dyfed is broken up into smaller administrative units?

'I think this sort of area and the ones nearer Swansea will revert back to English; perhaps Cardigan and the interior, the actual heartland and Lampeter will retain their Welsh essence. But if a child is brought up to speak Welsh, it will always speak Welsh. Had I come to live in Wales and married a Welshman who spoke fluent Welsh I'm sure my children would have been brought up to speak Welsh.

'There are so many who were born and bred in this area who don't speak a word of Welsh, the majority I would say, and the reason is because they haven't spoken it at home with their spouses. Consequently the kids are learning it at school, but it's a foreign language, it's exactly the same as if you were living in France, having to be taught English at school. It's this forcing of the language which I feel is wrong. It's these people who don't realize what it's like to have to go into a new community and learn a language who are propagating this culture. You must learn Welsh, you must learn Welsh. When you try to make people do things immediately you get a certain percentage who are resistant to it. I don't know what the answer is to it, but I don't think Welsh would die out, as long as it's spoken in the home. As soon as those kiddies in Llanddeusant get out in that playground, they're speaking in English; as soon as they get out in the playground in Llanwrda, they're speaking in English. Unless you can get them speaking Welsh in the playground you'll never keep the language.'

John Jones, Ystradgynlais, Powys*

A wet afternoon. John Jones is sheltering from the rain under the lych gate at St Cynog's in the centre of the village. He is fifty-four. Originally from Cwmllynfell, three miles across the border in Dyfed, he has lived in Ystradgynlais for the past twelve years, drawn by the need for work and his wife's family connections with the place. With him was his dog, Scooby.

'I was a miner, but now I work at Lucas SEI in Ystradgynlais, making harnesses for cars. It stands for Sumitomo Electrical Industries – Japanese, you know. I've been there five years as what they call a setter operator. There are about two thousand of us down there, a lot of them ex-miners. I got offered redundancy from Blaen Nant, didn't like it there. When Cynheidre closed and the men transferred from Cynheidre to Blaen Nant I got an offer to finish and so I did. I was on the dole for about ten weeks then I got this job down in Lucas. That was the only time I'd drawn the dole in my life. Others haven't been as lucky as me. I've got a son on the dole now. There's a lot round this area out of work. Apart from Lucas there's nothing else here; couple of shops of course and the industrial estate with about four, five, working in the units.

'I'm at home here. I'm in the choir – *Côr Meibion Ystradgynlais*. No, we don't compete in the Eisteddfod. There's two choirs in Ystrad, see: the little choir and the big choir. Ours is the big one; we've got about a hundred singers, and the little one, the Gerlais, has got about thirty-five. At the moment we're on our holidays; we've got a break now for about a month and then we start back to practices – every Wednesday and Friday evening – and then there's a programme of concerts. We go all over the place. I've been in, let's think now, Canada, America, I've been in Germany three times, Brittany, all with the choir. I sing baritone. I'm glad I'm with the choir. It's the best thing I've done, joining the choir and it's been a good . . . hobby, you know. Really good. Other than that . . . well, I used to play cornet in a brass band and tenor horn, years ago, like. So I could read music when I joined the choir and they prefer sol-fa and that's a lot easier anyway.

'I worked down the pit in Treforgan for ten years, that's where I started off. Treforgan closed just after the strike, you know, the '84 strike. I was on strike for a year. It was hard. A lot of the boys went off to picket up in England and places like that, but I was based here, I didn't go off at all. We used to meet at the Welfare Hall before they did it all up. On the Wednesday we used to get all the food in. There was a depot at the Banwen Miners' Hall, that's where all the food used to come from and then they'd transfer it to Cwm-twrch, Ystrad, then you'd go to Ystrad to fetch it. You'd get a bagful, you see. And that was a bit of a help anyway. There was no money coming in. You had to go picketing to get money. I remember Kim Howells here and Scargill was down, you know. I went to hear him in Port Talbot.

'And Scargill, you know, he was right in what he said. As the years went by, it was true. No doubt about it. They closed all the pits and the strike did nothing at all. It made no difference, like. He was spot on, but he went about it in the wrong way. This is my opinion, right? Well, Nottingham didn't come out to start with because there was no ballot and I think Scargill went about it the wrong way. We'd have liked a ballot, it would have been better, but they decided to come out and it finished up exactly like the 1926 strike, didn't it? Nottingham didn't come out with us and we were left on our own. And Margaret Thatcher had prepared for the strike. You know, she'd stockpiled coal and had paid for the police so we had no chance in a way. As the strike went on it got worse. We didn't have a hope.'

When did you realise it was hopeless?

'Well, the strike started in March and then in July when NACODS had their ballot to come out and then they turned back, you remember? They went back on their word. From then.'

How is the strike seen today?

'A lot of the men were angry with the police. I've not bothered with the police since the strike. The local police used to go away because they got paid more and we had them in from all over.

'And there was one miner living not far from here and he was the scab. Nobody has anything to do with him even now. He still lives in the same place, but the men have nothing to do with him, don't even speak to him. Say he goes to the pub, nobody bothers with him. And his wife the same. He went every in day, you see, from the first day for the whole year. There were a couple more later, like, but he went in from day one. And at the end of the strike he got a payment for being . . . faithful, like, extra on top of his redundancy.

'Through the strike the wife worked as a home help in the mornings to get money in, then in a chip shop in the afternoon, she came home and then off to the chip shop in the evenings . . . just to bring money into the house. I've got a girl and a boy. Well the boy was still at school, and the girl had started work so she helped with money. We managed to, what do you call it, not get into debt, you know, but hundreds of the boys went into debt and they're still paying it off today.'

Mary Ellen Jones, Cricieth, Gwynedd

Mary Ellen Jones is sixty-nine and has lived back in Wales for the past fifteen years, having spent all her working life in England. Despite being born in Uwchmynydd, Llŷn, she speaks with an almost imperceptible Welsh accent. She is active in Cynulliad Merched Cymru, *the Wales Assembly of Women.*

'I'm a native of Dwyfor, the far end of Llyn and in my early days it was the Welsh language only and so English is my second language, which I had to learn at the age of eight. I had no difficulty learning and I really mean that, although English wasn't heard very often . . . no difficulty. If you have a mind to learn I think you will. For all its obvious faults, Wales has always been keen on education. . . but then you have to go away to find employment because all those teachers, preachers, Wales couldn't possibly employ us all. So there was a tendency to move to the large cities. I came to the middle of my education during the War years which meant that you had to leave anyway . . . and I ended up in Liverpool. I was teaching for thirty-five years in Liverpool then moved back into Wales when I became a widow.

'I've always been very concerned about the image of older women. I believe that just because she retires that everything else about her doesn't retire; you know, her ability, her experience, her professionalism, she still has it and in these days of early retirement – and I retired early – retirement is a challenge rather than the other way around. I decided that I would do something for an agency that I've always admired, which is Oxfam. So right from 1979 I have been involved with Oxfam's campaign in education both here and overseas, and it is because of my role within Oxfam that I became aware of this group, the Wales Assembly of Women. The Chair of the of the local group in Gwynedd asked me if I would be a speaker on their International Day because of my experience working with women in Zambia. And I realised that *this* was the platform, reaching the National Council of Women and reaching government and finding a role for women. This is a valuable group, this is the voice of the women in Wales, all of the women. There's also the linkage, the global vision and rural women from the most rural areas of Wales definitely have a global vision. My Welshness gives me an added dimension. When I meet up with women of other minority groups anywhere in the world I really do believe that I am halfway there because what they are saying we have been saying or we have been feeling. The women of Wales are very important to me and wherever I go, here – and maybe next year I could be in Central America – I'm a Welshwoman, I'm a woman from Wales.'

Has your time in Liverpool sharpened your sense of Welsh identity?

'I've become very much aware that images are important and the image of the Welshwoman is of somebody with a black hat and a shawl and they don't see that we've got a variety of images. We have abilities, we have skills.'

At this point Mary Ellen Jones showed me a photograph she had taken in Bangkok of Welsh journalist Gwenda Richards standing next to a Thai woman.

'A Welsh woman reporter interviewing a Thai lady who has received the equivalent of the Nobel Peace Prize for her work with the urban poor, especially the women. And I can remember saying to her, "Are we really doing something by coming here?" And she said, "We couldn't really do without you." Then she said, "You are Welsh, you will understand that we are different." And I knew what she meant. She was educated up to the age of twelve and then did something similar to what I'm doing, she dedicated her life to improving the status of young women in Thailand. It was through her that we were actually able to go into the brothels, into the gay bars and to really learn the background. When you're not educated, when your family is on the breadline you are responsible for that family according to their tradition. What else can you do? So they end up going south, that's what they call it, and what we're trying to do is what she's trying to do – income generation to stop all this. I met her because we're part of her project, the Pratip Foundation. And that's where I, as a Welshwoman, was able to link with so many of these women and actually, literally sit on the ground with them.'

Neli Jones, Pontrhydfendigaid, Dyfed*

Neli Jones is a native of Pontrhydfendigaid and has lived there all her life. Married, with two daughters both in higher education, she plays an active part in local cultural life, what in Welsh is called 'y pethe'.

'I sometimes think I'm a bit too busy. I'm co-secretary of the Pantyfedwen Eisteddfod with my husband, Selwyn. He's done the job for the past eighteen years and I've helped him all that time and I'm officially his partner now. I'm also the treasurer because we can't get a treasurer at the moment. That's a bit of extra work. I'm a member of *Merched y Wawr* [*A woman's organisation, lit.* Daughters of the Dawn] and I've been organist at the chapel for the past twenty-five years, I think . . . no, thirty-five years! I've been a deacon for the past three years and a Sunday school teacher. I'm a piano teacher and I've got thirty-seven pupils at the moment. I present a programme on Radio Ceredigion every Sunday morning, a classical music programme. I'm a local reporter for *Y Barcud*, the *papur bro*. I believe in keeping busy. If I've not got enough to do I'm not happy.

'I'm a bit worried about incomers, to tell the truth. This village has changed quite a bit in the last few years. There's a drugs problem here at present. The local secondary school has had problems, you know, with pupils expelled from school. But it's just as busy as ever. There are still plenty of Welsh here. There are three teachers in the village school, and the majority of the children are Welsh-speaking. That's more than a lot of other villages in the area can say. Ysbyty Ystwyth is four, or five maybe, miles away and there's Swyddffynnon three miles in the other direction and they're . . . it's almost all English there. We're very fortunate, I suppose. The chapel's changed, too. We've lost a lot of the old regulars, elderly people. We've lost thirteen members since last year. We've got young people and they're very good and if there's a service for them themselves they're there and they're always ready to take part, but it's as if there's no one to take the place of the older ones. So I don't know what the future of the chapels and the church in the village is going to be.

'Like everything else, the audience for the Eisteddfod's gone down recently, too. The competitors are really good, I have to say. There's no shortage. We have had a shortage of choirs, choral competitions, but during the last two years it's as if the choirs are coming back now. We pay travelling costs now and more are coming. We had a choir over from Michigan two years ago, the whole way for the Eisteddfod, fair play. We've always had a bilingual policy in the Eisteddfod, you know, from the start, and in the early ones I felt that it was rather anglicised. One thing I remember is my husband, before we were married, came to do a recitation in the Eisteddfod, and he wasn't very pleased with all the English adjudications in the music competitions and he shouted out from the back of the pavilion, "*Cymraeg!*", you see? And two policeman took him out! This would have been back in nineteen-sixty something . . . 1970, around then. Well, this was on the Saturday, and he went back to the Eisteddfod on the Monday to do his recitation, to compete! He was afraid that he wouldn't be allowed to. Well, he got to compete and after that, when we got married, one of the first things that happened was that we got invited onto the committee and I think that after that to some extent we perhaps Welshified the Pantyfedwen Eisteddfod. It's not as anglicised now as it was. Sir David James, the founder, was born in Pontrhydfendigaid and he started the Eisteddfod with his money. We still get grants towards the prizes – eight or nine thousand a year, I think, from Pantyfedwen, the Pantyfedwen Fund. And because he spoke English I think that the first committees were held in English because he attended them and the Eisteddfod became anglicised. But by now it's very Welsh.

'Local *eisteddfodau* have made quite a contribution, I think, to the life of the area but more's the pity they're all coming to an end, the small ones. There aren't many left. Ours is a fair-sized one, but of the small ones, I think there's only Swyddffynnon left in this area, the St David's Day Eisteddfod. There was an eisteddfod in Ysbyty Ystwyth and in Pontrhydygroes and in Lledrod. But now there's only Swyddffynnon, Llanilar,

Ponterwyd . . . and Tregaron, of course. And these village *eisteddfodau* are important. Local children take part, all the schoolchildren, and sometimes one will go up on stage, children in the nursery school, and stand there and not say a word, but at least they've been on stage, you see.

'What cheers me most about Wales is seeing so many children learning Welsh, so many learners. I've done a lot with the Urdd Eisteddfod and that's full of learners. And what disheartens me? Well, in this village we've seen – I suppose I've got to speak from both sides – there are some parents who are willing to take part in everything even though they don't speak Welsh. They join in. There are others, we haven't seen them out of their houses more or less. They don't do anything in the village. That depresses me, to tell you the truth, that they buy houses and just go there to live and don't play any part in village life. If the young people stay I see quite a good future for Pontyrhydfendigaid. A lot of youngsters have to go away to work, but we're quite lucky because we seem to have plenty of young families with children here. And I just hope now that they can stay and take over from the older ones.'

Neville Hugh Jones, Prestatyn, Clwyd

Neville Jones appears to know – and be known by – the entire population of the town where he was born fifty-four years ago. He retired last year after a teaching career in Atherstone, St Asaph and, for twenty-six years, Prestatyn High School. He played football for the University of Wales as a student in Bangor and has represented the Prestatyn East ward on Rhuddlan Borough Council since 1979, standing as an Independent. He was Mayor of Prestatyn in 1984. One of three brothers, he is the only one still living in Wales.

'I love Prestatyn because I've worked on a very simple basis: PPP – Pleasant Prestatyn People, and as a teacher, Pleasant Prestatyn Pupils. I've had the *privilege* of living in Prestatyn, the *privilege* of teaching at Prestatyn High School. Ninety-nine point nine per cent of all my ex-pupils I regard as personal friends and I think they regard me as a personal friend.

'I'm a Manchester United supporter, have been since 1948. People say, "Why do you support United? You have no connections with Manchester" . . . I used to listen to the radio, football results on the radio, and I used to write down the names of the teams as I was listening to them, and of course it was in alphabetical order – and in those days it was Arsenal, Aston Villa, but then there was a host of Bs: there was Blackpool and Bolton; there was Blackburn, there was Birmingham, there was Burnley. And then you'd come to the Cs and it was Charlton. And I was writing these out as furiously as I could. As I say, I was only seven and I was writing with a pencil and it was going across the page and I couldn't get the second team in, I just had time to write the first, the home team. And I came to Manchester United. And I *couldn't* get it in one line. I thought, "Good God, what a big team". Fortunately for me – and fortunately for Manchester United – if I'd got down to the Ws I'd have been completely stuck, because West Bromwich Albion, I'm damned sure that I wouldn't have been able to spell it and I could have been a West Brom supporter from that point on if I'd been able to spell it. So it's Manchester United.

'I have a tremendous love of sport. I played rugby fleetingly, but one of the happiest parts of my life is the fact that I've been able to go to the two Home Internationals in Cardiff for the last twenty-five years . . . Cardiff Arms Park is so central. Like, Twickenham is miles out of the city, Murrayfield's miles out of the city, but Cardiff Arms Park is *absolutely* central and you can be in a pub and you can leave the pub at twenty-three minutes past two and, if you know which way to go, you can be in your seat at twenty-*eight* minutes past two. And I've always attempted to do that because I have never ever yet missed the Welsh National Anthem. And for anyone who's never been to Cardiff Arms Park and who's a Welshman or is any rugby supporter, to experience the Welsh crowd singing the Welsh National Anthem is something absolutely magic. I have never ever completed it yet. I've looked at the sky, I've looked at the concrete, I've looked at the players, I've looked at my neighbour, I've looked at my feet and I still never have got through it without my eyes absolutely *rolling* with tears and the bristles on the back of my neck standing. Especially when we get to *Gwlad, GWLAD, pleidiol wyf* . . . and I've been there so many times and I still yet haven't finished it. And I hope and pray that every time that I go that I still won't finish it.

'Prestatyn. As you drive up Prestatyn from the railway station, it's a single . . . people call it a one-horse town, it's a one-*street* town, with avenues radiating off the High Street. And as you go up High Street you get to the top and there is the pub called the Cross Foxes, which I believe dates back to the sixteenth century. And then if you go beyond that up Fforddlas you go up the one-in-four hill to Gwaunysgor, which is a beautiful village with a fantastic view of north Wales. You're able to see on a clear day the whole of Snowdonia. It's a panoramic thing, it's rather like looking at the Nevada Hills from the centre of the Nevada Desert.

'People who've lived here for a long time always regret that a beautiful place called Penisardre Farm, which is now a shopping precinct down at the bottom of town, has gone. And I'll say nothing other than to say that Prestatyn Urban District Council, whoever were responsible for the selling of that, really should be locked up. I deliberately haven't found out who were responsible because they may be still alive. That was a sixteenth-century farm and the owner was a fellow called Corbet Lloyd Ellis, who was a tremendous character and one of my abiding memories is when I lived in Glyn Avenue. What is now car parks were allotments and I was able to go through the allotments to go shopping for my mother, emerging into High Street. And on one Saturday in June 1952 I went into town to do some shopping for my mother and I beheld this brilliant sight. Prestatyn was of course building up as a holiday resort – why it built up as a holiday resort is that it's a geographical *fact* that from Point of Ayr to Llandudno the coastal strip has an average rainfall of twenty-five inches, which is the lowest in the country, vying with the English Riviera, i.e. Torquay. You get to Blaenau Ffestiniog and you've got a *hundred* inches of rain, but that's why Blaenau Ffestiniog is a slate town and Prestatyn is a holiday resort. So obviously it built up because it has a lovely climate and lots of people came here after the War and enjoyed their holidays and enjoyed the number of hours of sunlight. Thus Prestatyn and Rhyl have, with Eastbourne, the highest percentage of retired people in Britain.

'Now the person who owned Penisardre farm, Corbet Lloyd Ellis, was a town councillor on Prestatyn Urban District Council and he was a cantankerous fellow but a great character. And, apparently, from people who knew him in Council, if he'd decided on his own opinion, that was it. Black could be white and white could be black. And I like to think that he'd lost a vote in the Council – like fifteen-one – but he'd stood his ground and thus he was going to repay the people of Prestatyn, or the Council of Prestatyn. And this second Saturday in June 1952 I came onto the High Street and I saw Corbet driving his herd of pigs up the High Street. Pigs, as you know, are the most uncooperative of animals. He had two corgis and a sheepdog and his stick, he was roaring and shouting, the pigs were not cooperating and at that time, of course, there were no parking restrictions, and the High Street was two-way. There were cars parked on both sides, there were double-deckers going up, double-deckers coming down. Chaos. Of course, added to that were the pigs. And the pigs were grunting, squealing, excreting, going into every shop, knocking people down, knocking stalls down. But he relentlessly drove them up to Pendre Square, somehow miraculously turned them round and drove them back down. And there's only two or three people left in Prestatyn who ever witnessed that.

'I have firmly never believed that politics, national politics, should be involved in local councils. So I'm an Independent. There's an Independent group and there's a Labour group. We argue like hell with each other and yet we're the best of friends outside. And someone will say, "Well, why are you Independent?" Well, my parents were Liberal, I suppose when it comes to national politics I would vote Liberal, whatever was available – or Plaid Cymru. But when they say, "Why don't you involve politics in local government?" I say it's as simple as this. I represent three thousand people. If, for instance, the bin lorry, the Rhuddlan Borough bin lorry, skidded on an icy road and knocked someone's wall down and I was the Councillor, then I would go and represent that person *against* the Council, not the Council against the constituent. And I certainly wouldn't ask that person, "Did you vote for me? *Are* you Labour? *Are* you Liberal? *Are* you Conservative?" It has nothing at all to do with it. It's people, personalities. And that's where I come back to the Ps: People, Personalities, Public. And the reason I went on the Council was to give back some service to the town where I was born and bred, and to the people I love. I have, hopefully, served correctly and a lot of people know me and that is the benefit of being an Independent, whereby I can look someone squarely in the eye and say to them, "You've asked me to do something. I haven't asked any favour of you. I will do it for you because you're from Prestatyn. You love the area, I love the area and we're all friends together." PPP: Pleasant Prestatyn People. Politics doesn't come into it. P for politics doesn't come into it. Personalities do, pleasant natures do, people do. It's as simple as that. If I can continue to serve the people of Prestatyn and in the future the people of the re-vamped authority I will only be too pleased . . . I'm happy to be a Prestatyn person and I think Prestatyn's beautiful.'

Richard T. Jones, Penygroes, Gwynedd*

A knot of people are standing outside a terraced house a few yards up from the war memorial in Penygroes. The eldest of them, Dic Jones, is leaning on a walking-frame following a broken thigh a year earlier. He is eighty-eight. I am invited into a warm, large house, a former shop, for tea and conversation with him and his wife, Mary.

'I was born in Nebo, about two miles from here, in an old house called Glangors Uchaf. My father and grandfather and great grandfather were born in the same house, if not in the same bedroom. My grandfather on my mother's side was killed at Cwmorthin, the quarry in Ffestiniog. The bridge gave way under them and he and another man went down, leaving about ten children as orphans. There was one lad, Richard, the son of an uncle of mine, my mother's brother. He lived because he was lighter. Grandad was too heavy. My father died in 1936 with coal dust and slate dust on his lungs. He'd worked in the mines in Ferndale and Tylorstown and had come home in the summer to cut hay in Nebo.

'We've been married fifty-four years and so it's fifty-four years we've lived in this house. We've got three children: Delyth's the eldest, then Dylan, then Rhodri, he lives in Pentyrch, outside Cardiff. Then there are six offspring, three boys and three girls. Rhys is married and lives over the bridge here and we're expecting a great grandson or daughter in January.

Penygroes is still very Welsh. To the great credit of the education system in Gwynedd all the children learn Welsh, however distant their roots, and belong to the village. There's a doctor from Yorkshire who's learned Welsh fluently, fair play to him. All the chapels are Welsh. In every shop you get served in Welsh, with no *llediaith*, no pidgin Welsh, at all. Every policeman they send here can speak both languages. There's something special here, something uniquely Welsh. A lot of the English who come here turn Welsh. By and large, everyone who comes here from outside makes an effort with the language . . . and the way of life, that's important, isn't it? A neighbourly way of life. We had a neighbour here last night for a good part of the evening boasting that this was a good neighbourhood. She said that there were a hundred shops here in the past. There are very few now, but they're good ones. There are four chapels, two belonging to the *Hen Gorff*, the Methodists, one Congregationalist and one Baptist. The Wesleyan closed a bit since. That's the religious side. There's a flourishing literary society.

'I'm very hopeful for the future of Penygroes from the linguistic point of view. It's a pity that there isn't more work, but the look of the village is very tidy and I'm confident about the village's future through it all. We've relied almost completely on the slate industry and that's been lost, but the majority of people haven't lost heart. Whenever I go away, I'm always pleased to come back to Penygroes.'

He excuses himself for not showing me to the door.

Roy Baker Jones, Solva, Dyfed

Born in Cardiff to Welsh parents, father from Cardiganshire, mother from Swansea, Roy was brought up in Canada. A ten-year career in pop music made him enough money to buy and renovate a cottage in Solva seven years ago. He has just graduated in English from Swansea and is hoping to get funding to do a Masters degree on Dylan Thomas. We are speaking in the giftshop at St David's Cathedral where he has a holiday job with Cadw.

Did you know this area of Wales before you moved here?

'No, I don't think I really knew it. I had this kind of idealised conception of what it was like because I'd spent all my time here in holiday mode, walking round the cliffs or down the pub and all that, but in terms of the reality of the work situation I didn't have a clue.

'I've found a Wales, I've found my Wales. It's not all good and it's not all bad. It's the people that you meet. It's how you're forced to live because of the economic conditions. It's a sort of atmosphere. I was learning to speak Welsh when I was living in London doing a courier's job, driving round the streets and trying to learn because I'd always had a very strong feeling for Wales since I was a child. To a certain extent, for me it was like trying to discover what I might have lost by the fact that my parents moved away from Wales when I was young. There was a mystery about the language because they spoke to each other in Welsh when we were children, but we couldn't understand them so they always gave the Welsh language this mystery. I've been studying Welsh on and off for ten years and I'm still not fluent, you know. I can understand a lot now, but I still can't speak fluently. It's only in the last year or so that people have actually been speaking Welsh to me. Or maybe that was my own inhibitions, thinking that my Welsh was too stilted or was too book-learnt. I wouldn't take the plunge and make a fool of myself in front of people. But since I've started doing that I've found that people have sort of responded. That's been quite positive.

'I'm a musician and I've found that when I lived in England everything was very ambitious – all the projects I was involved in were aimed at making money – whereas the creative projects I get involved in now are just for their own sake because there isn't the sort of expectation of success in Wales. But that's not a problem. I think that enhances the quality of what you do. I think that applies to everything. I mean, the standard of living isn't as high here as it is in the south of England, but that doesn't mean that the quality of life is worse. Particularly in an area like this you've got so much beauty around you all the time, but you can't find work. It's very hard to get work and the work here is very low-paid. You've just got to accept that. If you don't, then you know you'll just have a bad time.'

How has working in a giftshop like this affected your view of Wales?

'I was listening to a programme on Radio 4 this morning saying that in Scotland their marketing people are trying to get away from the haggis and kilts sort of thing and trying to bring over more of what the people of Scotland are actually about . . . and that this is the real wealth of the country – the people – rather than this kind of cartoon image that American tourists have got of what Scotland is. *Cadw* seem to be on very much the same lines: they've got this campaign, called "Makers of Wales", which is trying to bring to the attention of people who are coming to Wales what the people are actually doing with their lives, what actually happens in Wales rather than the knotwork and Celtic mysticism, the *Mabinogion* – not that there's anything wrong with all that. In the shop we've had all this stuff – the "Makers of Wales" – but no-one is buying it. People are still going for all the old stuff that they've been selling for years. It's probably because of the setting down here; there's the Bishop's Palace and the Cathedral. The sort of people who come here are probably looking for more of a mystical experience rather than an experience of Welsh people . . . the sort of Welsh people that you meet in the Valleys or whatever. I mean, I've been meeting more people like that in Swansea; and that's a completely different side of Wales again. It's almost like a different world again within Wales. There is something uniting the two things, but I don't know what exactly. I think it's a kind of humility or something and a scorn of things that are ostentatious. Like a desire to get to the root of something and not embellish it and make it seem something greater than it really is. That's a trait both in the Valleys and Pembrokeshire. And heritage? I think it's a good move that the general trend should be moving away from the knotwork and moving towards realising what life is actually like for the people who are living here.'

Behind the shop is filling with a coachload of Americans. Roy wraps a swathe of brown paper around a doll in national costume.

Huw Meirion Lewis, Llangefni, Gwynedd*

Huw Meirion Lewis was born on a farm in Glanrafon, Bala and gives his age as 'sixty-five plus'. He is tall and bespectacled, with a slight scholar's stoop. I met him taking a rest by the clock in Bangor town centre during a shopping trip with his wife, Gwenno. He was educated at Ysgol Tŷ Tan Domen, Bala, then spent two years in the Air Force, before going to Bangor to read Electrical Engineering.

'Jobs in engineering were relatively difficult to come by locally, so I took a post with GEC in Coventry. I was there for four years. It was in Coventry in fact, through the Welsh Society, that I met Gwenno. We were married in 1956 – in Welsh – by the Presbyterian minister, JR Owen. Gwenno was north Walian, but, being a minister's daughter herself, she had no ties with any one place in particular. Coventry in the fifties had a thriving Welsh community – Welsh services, social events and the rest of it. I was secretary for a while, but I missed the pace of life in Wales, I suppose, and we were determined to go home when the opportunity arose.

'Well, as luck would have it, later that same year I was offered a job at Ferranti in Port Dinorwic. We jumped at the chance. Never regretted it, of course, but, to tell you the truth, it was a bit of an anti-climax when we first moved back to Wales. The Welsh Society in Coventry had been so close, you see, and suddenly we found ourselves hardly knowing anyone. The following year the firm moved to Llangefni and I moved with it and we set up home in Anglesey.

'I left Ferranti's in 1961. There were two reasons really. First, there was a danger that I might be made redundant, and second, I had an urge to go back into the academic world. I took my teacher's certificate and for five years I taught physics at Ysgol John Bright in Llandudno. No, I didn't move. I commuted – how far would it be? Thirty miles each way – between Llangefni and Llandudno every day. It was quite a change after working on my own doorstep.'

Gwenno joins us. How has Llangefni changed in the thirty-five years or more since they moved there?

'Probably for the worse. There are so many empty shops there now. The High Street is definitely – how shall I put it? – well, let's say less attractive than it was. And you hear stories about a drugs problem. Llangefni's got quite a reputation for that sort of thing.'

Gwenno says that she wouldn't want to walk through the town alone after dark. They agree that the press probably sensationalise the matter, but still feel uneasy.

'Are you taking all this down? Llangefni's still a nice place to live. Can you put that? There are lots of worse places. Let's say that it's *comparatively* less attractive than it was. There are good things about it.'

An old friend comes by. Huw Lewis finds himself torn between us, grateful perhaps for the interruption. 'I wouldn't live anywhere else,' *he concludes.* 'Put that, will you?'

Fiona Liddell, Libanus, Brecon, Powys*

Dr Fiona Liddell is originally from Birmingham and has lived in Wales for the past three and a half years. Her husband, a minister in the United Reformed Church, is a Welsh-speaking Cardiffian. She works for the Health Promotion Trust in Brecon. The entire interview was conducted in Welsh in the Learners' Tent at the Neath Eisteddfod.

'I started to learn because of my husband originally, but we've got a one year-old daughter now and she's a great spur for me. We want to bring her up bilingually. Also, I want to be fluent. In the beginning it's hard to express yourself properly. I say the nearest thing rather than what I really want to say. We try to speak Welsh at home. Every now and again, of course we turn to English because it's easier for us . . . for me at least!'

How well did you know Wales before moving here to live?

'I knew some parts from my childhood holidays. Wales is a popular holiday place for people from Birmingham. Particularly Pembrokeshire . . . Colwyn Bay . . . the Brecon Beacons. But I didn't appreciate the culture as being in any way different, or the different traditions. I suppose that I must know the Welsh better now. The most important thing was getting to know my husband. He's very pleased that I'm learning. He was very keen for me to start. But now I try to explain to him that it's not because of him that I'm carrying on learning. Especially here in the Eisteddfod. I well remember the first time I went to an Eisteddfod with him before we got married and I didn't understand a word. But every time I've come back I've got more out of it. Now I say to him, "Look, I want to go to such and such a place." I'm happy to meet people now without him. At the start he knew everyone and I was introduced as his wife or his friend.'

Do you think you'll always be a learner? Do you foresee a time when you will have 'crossed the bridge' to fluency and independence in Welsh?

'I've crossed one big bridge just this year, since having the baby. I had a full year away from work, so there was time to read, listen to the radio and talk to my daughter. An important psychological bridge. A year, no, six months ago, I wouldn't have been happy to be interviewed without having prepared. But now I have had the chance twice to do interviews with Elin Rhys on radio. The first was in February. I was very nervous, but my husband said, "Oh, you'll be alright." He was in on the thing so there was a chance to prepare and ask him for different phrases. The subject for once wasn't learning Welsh; it was women and mental health.'

Are you tired of being a learner?

'Not yet. I've just done the "Use of Welsh" test this June and now I'm aiming at something higher. I'm also looking forward to reading a book just for ordinary people and not specifically for learners. And I've not reached that level yet. But it'll come.'

At the conclusion of the interview she gestures relief by theatrically mopping her brow. 'Thanks for the practice,' *she says.*

Brychan Llŷr, Blaenannerch, Cardigan, Dyfed*

Brychan Llŷr Jones was born twenty-four years ago into a south Cardiganshire farming family, son of the poet Dic Jones. He now performs with the Welsh rock band Jess.

'I was involved in music through primary school, in shows, operas, choirs, competing in the Eisteddfod and so on, like most Welsh children. Then after going to secondary school in Cardigan and meeting Emyr, we used to talk during our first couple of years there – when I was eleven, twelve – about forming a band. I can't remember where I'd got the idea from, but that's what we wanted to do, both of us. Our chance came, then, when we were going through Fourth Year because my sister was selling musical instruments, living in Cardiff . . . involved in these things. So we spent all the money I'd saved, spent it on amps and keyboards and so on and an electric guitar and from then on we started the band and Chris came to us after that – he was at the same school, too, a year older than us – and that was the backbone of the group. We met Owen when our drummer, the original one, had to leave the band. He was the same age as us, he'd been at school with us, but his mam and dad wanted to send him to college. So Owen joined us and that's how Jess was formed.

'I'd say that Wales has two musical worlds: the more formal, classical one and the contemporary one. I'm part of the second category, but I'd say that things are quite a bit healthier in the first because there's a lot more competition and people take it a lot more seriously. You don't get people wasting other people's time, turning up to play concerts without having practised. You get a lot of that in contemporary music, where you get bands performing on stage in television programmes who don't deserve, really, to be there at all. Because they get the chance to go on television just because they sing in Welsh. The situation was even worse three, four years ago than it is now. There aren't enough television programmes creating enough money now to support Welsh groups, so groups are having to go out and play live concerts . . . that is, the groups who really want to do it. So the situation's a little bit healthier. But the world of Welsh rock is a very *small* one. There's not that much money to be made in it, so if you want to be professional and support yourself entirely through music you've got, I think, to look beyond Offa's Dyke for your bread and butter. In the Welsh rock world it's a pity really that it's also so . . . how shall I put it? . . . not everybody's out to help each other. With something so small it could easily be like that, but there's a lot of people who go about their business in quite an . . . unpleasant way, I think; they don't make things any easier for others. But there it is, it's not an easy business.

'By now *Jess* works outside Wales a good bit more than it does within Wales. For example, this year I think that we've done something like four, perhaps five concerts in Wales and outside Wales we must have done, I don't know, thirty, forty concerts. We're also working with Mike Peters at the moment. It's not something I foresee going on for ever because we want to do our own music, ideally, and I think it's something that will end quite quickly. Even so, we'll still have to work in England. London, next to Cardiff, is the city we've played in most and that suits me because the place excites me and I get quite a kick out of going there, not to mention going on stage and performing. By now we've played some quite large venues, for example the Empire Theatre, Shepherds Bush . . . I've been exceptionally lucky to go with Mike Peters and play there. I've not played there with *Jess* yet, but that day will come very soon, I'm sure.

'As *Jess*, we're not turning our backs on Wales and we never would, because we are Welsh. Although the drummer doesn't speak Welsh he comes from a Welsh background and he considers himself a Welshman. And so we will always consider ourselves to be a Welsh band. We'll always perform in Wales, always perform in Welsh. *Jess* is a Welsh band.'

James Lucas, Machynlleth, Powys

We are standing at the top of the funicular which carries one hundred thousand visitors annually the eighty feet or so from the car park up to the Centre for Alternative Technology. James Lucas, in his mid-twenties, has a holiday job on site. He was born in Peterborough to Welsh parents from Goginan near Aberystwyth.

'My father was in the RAF. I went to boarding school, primary and secondary. We moved around the country and Europe with the RAF, and settled down in Wrexham. I met a lady friend, whom I'm living with, who lives in Machynlleth and that's the reason why I'm here. At the present moment I'm studying Illustration in Wrexham Art College and I'm working here at the Centre as a summer job, basically, but hoping actually to get a permanent staff position here on the marketing team.

'The Centre is an excellent place to work. Being co-operative work it's pretty much ahead of the rat race. Upon finding it, I found it was a great ethos. It's fun to work here, the people here are great. The people locally are too. It's very Welsh-speaking round here, but it isn't a problem. They're either-or. Life's great; clean air, beautiful countryside, lots to do if you're into walking or sightseeing or bird-watching or fishing – and of course being local I haven't got far to travel for work . . . It's very safe. There's no crime to speak of, there's no outside influences, you know, hard drugs, disruptive youths or anything like that. There's very little crime, very little car crime. You can still leave the keys in your car. You can leave your door open. It feels safe, you feel secure. If you're willing to get on with the locals, they're very willing to get on with you, but they are the people if you cross . . . well, you don't want to do it.

'You have mountains all around you, you have pine forests and lots of sheep. Usually the weather's terrible, but the scenery makes up for it when it's good.

'I worked for ten years in the tourist industry before I went to college. I ran a caravan park outside Wrexham. And I ran my own section in previous jobs. I've always held junior management or management positions ever since leaving school, really. I suppose I was lucky. And I think I have a lot to offer the Centre, because at the moment they've been having a bit of trouble with the attendances and I think I could help through my PR skills and my general relating to the general public and that's why I want to help out, basically. I want to help. I want to help the *cause*, if you know what I mean, that we do here. Like I say, the whole ethos of it is wonderful and of course the goals that they do achieve, not just in this country but abroad, in the Third World and in other places, remote places in Scotland, some places in Wales, they do a wonderful job. And it's something that people should wake up and realise and get told about and so long as that learning process is fun I think it will spread and people will eventually realise. It'll be a long trek, but eventually they will see the importance of all this and I want a part of it, I really do. I want to be part of the pioneering team!'

Dilwyn Mathias, Carmarthen, Dyfed*

The Black Horse in the centre of Carmarthen is now called Y Ceffyl Du *and is a popular meeting place for Welsh-speaking students at Trinity College. During the summer the locals return. Dilwyn Mathias, fifty-nine and unemployed, has drunk there regularly since returning to Wales a year ago. I met him over a last pint before he went home explaining that he was 'afraid of the dark and the wife'.*

'I was in the army for twenty-two years, left and got work in Heathrow as a cargo serviceman. After fifteen years in Heathrow I came back to Wales and Carmarthen and since coming back I haven't seen any work at all. It's miserable. I'd take anything, anything tidy, but nothing working for anyone who wants to make money out of *me* . . . what's the word? . . . exploit me. My wife's here and my stepdaughter. My own kids are in Runcorn in Cheshire. I don't want to move any more. I've travelled the world and now I don't want to leave Carmarthen.

'Wales gets the worst of it. Definitely. Go to England, there's more work to be had, men in England are looked after. Come back to Wales and nobody cares about you. There's no work to be had, no work being offered, they treat you like . . . like a dog. There's no answer to it. The government has ruined this country and it's getting worse by the day, by the day.

Was it easy to settle back here?

'No, not really. I've been away too long. But it was the best thing to do, I think. I got early retirement in Heathrow and the best thing was to come back to Carmarthen. I had to come back to Carmarthen because my wife was here. When I was in England I spoke Welsh every evening over the phone to her. There were lots of Welsh working in Heathrow, not many spoke Welsh, but lots of Welsh people . . . You know what was the best thing that ever happened to me? I was in Cyprus, in the army, and I met a lad from Tumble and we had a chat together in Welsh for about three minutes. In Cyprus. It only lasted about three minutes, speaking Welsh, but it was wonderful, you know, speaking Welsh to someone out in Cyprus. I've never forgotten it.'

Cedric Morgan, Saundersfoot, Dyfed

After nearly six years in the RAF, serving in Singapore and Malaya, Cedric Morgan returned to Pembrokeshire in the late nineteen-fifties. He worked as a mechanic in local quarries and drove a crane during the construction of the power station at Pembroke Dock. He is now harbour master in Saundersfoot. We are talking in his office above the Harbour Commission with a view east to Worm's Head twenty miles away. The desk is piled with paper and a ship's radio which squawks intermittently throughout our conversation. Memorabilia share the walls with posters explaining safety procedures at sea. In 1972 Cedric Morgan took on the fish market in the town.

We run that and I went trawling mainly, doing my own fishing, serving my own market. Even with trawling you've still got to buy a certain amount of stuff. Obviously you can't catch kippers and smoked fish and prawns, but otherwise with the wet fish I kept the market going very well. I changed my boat on various occasions – I went bigger and I came down smaller. The trouble with fishing, if you go bigger the scale of your gear gets bigger, your fuel bills gets bigger, insurance is heavier, wear and tear is a lot heavier, so it don't always work out.'

He points to a framed photograph on the wall.

'That is my last vessel there. She's still here but she don't look like that now. That was a very successful boat. She was thirty-six feet. That's *Rosalinde*, named after the railway engine that plied along the harbour here for the coal trade. *Rosalinde*. About ten years ago – just over ten years ago – I took over as harbour master here. Hopefully . . . I'm sixty-five now in April, whether I will have to retire at sixty-five I can only leave to my superiors. I don't know that. I don't know how you see me, but I don't feel sixty-five, I feel fifty. And I'm quite capable of carrying on, but we don't know. I think sometimes you've got to draw a line somewhere and say well, somebody else should get a chance. There's no other reason for wanting to get rid of me because I'm popular with people. There's things I could quote, but I'd better not. I'm well known with the yachtsmen round the coast as far . . . well up the Severn, Briton Ferry, Ilfracombe, Milford Haven, up as far as Porthmadog – yachts'll come in – they all know Cedric. They're always welcome. It's very rare I'll turn a yacht away and only then when I turn one away it's when we're properly full and he comes in with a tall, thin keel which you can't accommodate them for the safety of the boat.

'My job is basically looking after the public, overseeing things, making sure that people are on the correct moorings, doing the right thing. We have a dory down here, a small dory with an outboard on, quite fast, with "Harbour Master" along the side. Now, we have to keep the beaches clear of idiots with ski-bikes, water-skiing. Very difficult to do. We had a meeting about it last week and I said if we've got them going out away from us, we've won. My thing is this beach, keep them out of there. I go out to these people and they are told in no uncertain terms, "Now look. These are the rules. Now, if you continue to do what you're doing now you will be asked to go into the beach. Now, you could be met by the police – or if you take your boat away, fair enough." But we can prosecute. Most people are very fair and say, "Sorry, we didn't know," but . . . those are the marker buoys. Look at those yellow buoys, they're just beyond low water right across here, do you see? Now all activities above a certain speed has got to be out there. Now, alright, a speedboat doing six or seven knots makes a hell of a wash, but that's nothing, the wash – it's the speed I'm concerned about. 'Come end of the season it's a matter of tidying up and then I have the – what can I say? – *unpleasant* task of servicing all the mooring chains in the harbour. It's an every-winter job. There's ninety-four moorings in the centre and we've got ninety-one on the perimeter – lot of chain. And you take the centre moorings, each chain is on the average forty to forty-five feet long – some of it's quite hefty. The further back we go on the harbour the bigger the chain; you've got to go up to twenty-two millimetre for that, because it takes all the waft if there's a storm. As you come up you can come down to half-inch and that's adequate for small boats. You've got to watch you don't under-do chain because they do come out and you have to change them more often. If you put them too heavy – a small boat – it might pull her under when the tide is high. We've had tides come running up actually round this building – that's no exaggeration – twice. I've had wet feet coming up here. As you see it now, it's beautiful, but you get a blow and a big tide and then you've got to start to think to yourself, God I hope I have done the chains properly, I hope by God they've got decent boats out there. The danger is if something happens to one boat – a boat breaks adrift – you've got to *try* and do something about it. Now you can't always and you can't do it yourself. You've got to have help.

'Although I was born in Plymouth, my parents were from here. My father was brought up in Saundersfoot as a lad, my mother was from Pembroke Dock, part of the famous Colley family. Now he travelled as a Singer sewing-machine man with a bike. He was their rep in this area. Only a real local will know certain things . . . if you say, "Where do you live?" "Oh, down the Larket", now, if you're not from here you don't know what the hell that means. The Larket is slang for Lower Cart. It's now called Westfield Road.

'Gradually things are getting worse as regards fishing. Fishing is going down, down, down. I think when I left the fishing industry, I think the fish went with me. There was a man, well known to this area although he's a Milford man, Jack Sinclair, he used to leave here and the fish used to go with him. Now Jack Sinclair taught me a lot about fishing. There's another man who gave me a lot of knowledge on the setting of nets, I think he's still in Carmarthen, he was running a pub there, Hughie Morgan, we called him Hughie Salmon. He taught me how to really set a trawl net – and if a trawl net is not set correctly it don't fish. Not a fish in there. Now as regards the prawning, in the rocks, and the lobstering – now I'll go back ten years now – you could go over to Monkstone Point and you could come home with half a bucket of nice prawns or a lobster. With the saturation fishing we have now and netting going on, I think it's killed it off. I went over twice this year and I don't think I've filled a good pudding basin full of prawns this year. It's as bad as that. They're not there any more for some reason.

Whether there's more pollution in the area than we realise and we're not being told – there are tests being taken all the time. When I see any problems I call in the NRA and tests are immediately taken; there are weekly tests. If there's a problem and they think it's something to do with the sewers then they call in the Water Authority and it is looked at immediately. There is no messing because we have to be very fussy about our beaches.

'It's very helpful as a harbourmaster to be a licensed boatman, to have been a fisherman. If you are going to sea and you ask me advice, I can tell you what the bottom's like, pretty well what the depth is like, the effects of the wind in certain areas. I can give you good advice in the immediate area of about twenty miles or further maybe. Not only that, if somebody comes in with a rope, if I have got time, I'll splice it for them!'

Julie Morson and Gemma Addicott, Builth Wells, Powys.

Julie Morson is small and her short dark hair frames her face. Her friend Gemma Addicott is taller with long, fair hair. They're talking on a damp bench in Builth, each taking turns but looking at each other in silent consultation before speaking. Both are fourteen.

Julie: It's alright living in Builth, it's quite quiet and everything, but I suppose it's alright to bring people up in. When the Royal Welsh Show comes here, there's more people and it's good for people to see Builth and Wales and that.
Gemma: It's OK, it's better on weekends because there's more to do. We go to dances when they're on, in Builth. They're quite good, we sometimes get live bands, but it's usually like a disco.
Julie: There's not that much to do round here. Sometimes there's the Youth Club on Tuesdays and Fridays, there's not really that much to do, just hang round town and that, a few people meet up and everything. It's quite a safe town.

What do you think of school?

Julie: It's alright. It's quite a nice school actually because it's all done out and not too many people in it. It's no so bad. It's got quite a good reputation.

Does Builth feel like part of Wales?

Julie: It doesn't seem too much, like, Welsh, because there aren't too many . .
Gemma: . . .Welsh-speakers . . .
Julie: . . .yeah, no Welsh-speakers. In Llanwrtyd Wells, just thirteen miles away, there's quite a few Welsh-speakers there, but hardly any in Builth and we're closer to England.

What are your plans for the future?

Gemma: I want to be a cetologist, working with dolphins and whales.

Julie: I hope to go away, maybe work on a cruise ship or something like that and maybe come back to Builth in the future, when I'm a bit older.'

Out of the darkness a group of boys come in our direction. A voice carries over. 'What you doing, Julie?' 'We're talking about Wales . . . for a book. You know, like the country and everything?' 'But it's bloody raining,' the voice remarks, already moving away.

Kathryn Nash, St Asaph, Clwyd *

Kathryn is standing at a piano in the empty dining room at Neuadd John Morris-Jones, the Welsh hall of residence at University College, Bangor. In a soprano voice she half practises, half performs a Welsh folk song, striking chords or single notes occasionally to guide herself. She is twenty and has just finished her second year.

'I was born in St Asaph. My dad's from Denbigh and works in livestock and my mum's a lecturer in the radiography department in Wrexham. My mum doesn't speak Welsh, but I went to Ysgol Glan Clwyd in St. Asaph. When I finished GCSEs I couldn't make my mind up between the sciences, or music, Welsh and history. In the end I chose arts. I'm doing a degree in Welsh and Media now and enjoying every minute of it. I thought I'd have difficulties because we speak English at home, but by now I don't feel out of it at all. I feel that Welsh is now my first language. There are learners in hall, but they're treated just the same as everyone else.

'I think that friends influenced me to be more Welsh. At the end of my third year at secondary school I could see myself going either way. I had two sets of friends at the time, one who spoke mostly English and the other mostly Welsh. And something – in my subconscious, I suppose – attracted me to the Welsh side.

'Another influence was the Young Farmers' Clubs locally. I didn't have a rural upbringing, but I feel comfortable in that sort of company because of my dad's connections. I really believe that in my area it's agriculture that's kept the language alive. People bringing up huge families, five children and more, all Welsh-speaking – the *Mudiad Magu Mwy* [Procreation Organization]!

'I don't know about the future. I'm pretty certain that I'll end up teaching Welsh in a secondary school, with a bit of drama, to make use of the media side of my degree. Yes, I know it's a very common choice for Welsh graduates. I've considered the media, too, but it's a matter of luck more than anything. It seems to be more who you know than what you know. Something to do with music would be good, too. I did Music as a subsid and I compete in *eisteddfodau*. The Inter-College Eisteddfod's in Bangor next year and I'm really looking forward to that. The hall is a very musical place. Everyone seems to sing or do something. I come from quite a musical family: my auntie sings a bit and my dad's got a good voice, but doesn't make enough of it.'

Would you consider travelling to get work?

'To south Wales, you mean? Yes, I would. I suppose that nowadays it's a matter of having to. Clwyd's a difficult place for new appointments and a lot of people from Clwyd are going after jobs in Gwynedd, so that creates a shortage here. To tell the truth, I don't really know south Wales. But I wouldn't be over-worried about going there. I'd be back up here in the long run.'

And outside Wales?

'I'd go. Again, if I could be certain that I could come back. I've got a friend who's at Oxford. Although she's thoroughly Welsh, she says that she appreciates the opportunity to meet so many new people. She misses Wales terribly, but she looks on it as the chance of a lifetime. I'd consider going further than England, just as long as I could get back eventually. To be honest, I'd go to Scotland or Ireland before going to England, given the choice.

'A lot of people say, if you're going away to university why don't you go a long way? Well, I'm half an hour away from home here, and that's far enough – out of sight of Mam. We don't have much to do with the English students in College. I only know a handful, to be honest. In hall there are a lot of the same type of people, the same background and so on. There are language differences between us and south Walians, but that's about it. I'm not sure if it's an advantage to be so close to home or not. In a way it is, because you can identify with people and feel at home straightaway. Something tells me that I was right to come to Bangor, but sometimes I think, what if . . ? I went down to see my friend in Oxford and life there seemed so interesting. You come across types of people you never meet here. For example, gays and lesbians. They're completely unknown to us in hall. When my friend came over from Oxford to see me, in a way *she* was jealous because of the Welsh atmosphere. But she's also very ambitious. She wants to be a professional harpist, so she's where she should be to meet the right people. Here, it's nice and relaxed.

'Wales means everything to me. Everything in my personality comes out of my Welshness. The language has given me something to care for and fight for. Welsh culture's important, too. If you don't speak Welsh, you miss out culturally.'

In what way?

'I'd say, for me, Young Farmers, Sunday school, chapel and – definitely – *eisteddfodau.*'

Geoffrey Pritchard, Merthyr Tydfil, Mid Glamorgan

Pritchards Estate Agents occupies a prime site in the centre of Merthyr Tydfil, on Market Street. Geoffrey Pritchard, its owner, is speaking to me in a small office with a large aerial photograph of the town on the wall.

'I was born in Merthyr Tydfil and was educated here at the local grammar school. At the time, being a war baby of 1940, when you were seeking a career in the early fifties there didn't seem to be a great deal of choice and you were guided towards the teaching profession or something similar. We seemed to export a lot of teachers from Wales – that and water. I, however, wanted to be something different and I resolved that I would have a job or a profession that took me indoors and out of doors. There was the dilemma. But for some reason or another I became friendly with a surveyor who *looked through a theodolite.* It seemed to be very attractive to me, so during my holiday periods I helped out. But for some strange reason I ended up being a chartered surveyor and a valuer. I vowed I would never be an estate agent, but here I am: a valuer, a chartered surveyor and an estate agent. And I'm now fifty-four. In my early years I was a student in London, then I worked in London, I worked for British Rail, I worked for a major firm in Cardiff and achieved the pinnacle of being a valuation surveyor – worked for the Inland Revenue District Valuers' Office. And that was the *crème de la crème,* or so I thought. And I was there for some five years. It was very good experience. I did realise, however, that I couldn't be a civil servant; their attitude to life was too rigid, and what I really wanted to do was to help people. It got to a point where I decided to set up on my own, and it was quite an effort in that I was then twenty-nine years of age, I'd been qualified about six years, married, small child, not a lot of money, a mortgage. But with the support of my wife and family I did this. I cut all ties with the Inland Revenue and opened up on the fourteenth of July 1969 – Bastille Day – in a little office in Merthyr Tydfil, without a case, without a house, without anything. Just a lot of determination and an overdraft. Here I am, twenty-five years on, with a *bigger* office, a *bigger* overdraft . . . ! But I feel I've enjoyed life and that I've helped the people of Merthyr. The type of work *I'm* doing at the moment is very much that of compensation valuation and putting together new development sites, new retail sites.

'The housing market in the Merthyr Tydfil area as of today is still very iffy. The housing stock in Merthyr Tydfil is still predominantly pre-1940s; there is a reasonable amount of modern property and there is an unusual trend at the moment for people to buy brand new houses. I don't mean second-hand modern houses, but brand new. We've analysed this as the desire of the female of the species when looking around the show house – because it is a policy of developers to have a *show* house – which they furnish and decorate and which really appeals to the female of the species, who wants *that* house. And we have found as agents over the years that we can sell the show house twenty times over, but the adjoining house which isn't decorated the same nobody wants. There is this trend: I want a new house. It has to be some form of desire for change.

'Merthyr is undoubtedly expanding. There's a lot of money being put into the town by the Welsh Development Agency: infrastructure, roads, new sites. The new A470 extension road is bringing a great deal of commercial interest into the town, and perhaps I'm a little more privileged than others in that I'm aware of these proposed developments, planning applications, interest by outside firms. I feel that the prosperity of Merthyr Tydfil is definitely on the increase. By the year 2000 we will see an entirely different Merthyr Tydfil to that of today.

'The prosperity of Merthyr is partly an accident of location. The A470 extension, which is the Cardiff, eventually Llangwryd, trunk-road is at the moment in the process of being extended. In one way it by-passes Merthyr, but the most important thing is, it brings trade, business and industry into the town. It's a fact that when they used to hang people in the old days they did it at a crossroads because it kept away the evil spirits. And somebody had the bright idea of shoeing your horse and selling you a pint of ale. That's the way the villages and the towns grew up. Merthyr is in very much that location. The Heads of the Valleys road – which is three-lane but will eventually become four-lane – connects us very quickly with the Midlands. The new A470 connects us with the M4 and we can virtually in Merthyr now get on a motorway to *anywhere*. We are very lucky in that respect. This is really what's bringing industry – and I mean industry, not just commercials – *into* Merthyr. South Wales as a whole suffered very much from the fact that the former coal industry and iron industry and heavy industries have now gone. They dwindled and dwindled over a period. They were substituted to some degree by light industry, engineering . . . but that's been superseded by technology. What we're aiming for in Merthyr – and what I think the WDA are aiming for, and outside parties are looking to bring into Merthyr – are high tech. skills. I think these will come to Merthyr and I think because of its asset as a location and road communication, Merthyr will survive where other Valleys towns, such as the Rhondda, Tredegar and even as far as Ebbw Vale – which have at the moment very little going for them – are not likely to survive.

'I think Merthyr will have to be shaken. The Merthyr *people* will have to have more pride in their town and not feel that, because they read the *Merthyr Express* – which is ninety per cent doom and gloom, crime and terror – that that is the bulk of Merthyr. It is not.

'If I have a concern about Wales, I think it's not so much for the physical aspect of the towns, it's for the future of the next generation. The education system in Wales is probably as sound as you would find anywhere – perhaps with the exception of the south east of England – but the opportunities to specialise are very, very limited, I feel, in Wales. The only example I can give is that of my daughter, playing violin and going to the Royal Academy this year. If we had not assisted her in getting the best private lessons possible, she probably would not have reached her ambition in being a member of the National Youth Orchestra for Wales. The bulk of the members are from the south Wales area and very few are from north Wales. Even fewer seem to be from the farming community of Wales. I feel this is indicative that if you're prepared to pay for your child's education – or supplement the existing system – there is a better opportunity of getting on. Serious thought and consideration must be given to the youth of Wales, because the youth of today are the future.'

Janet Rawlings, Chepstow, Gwent

Born in New Jersey and brought up in Connecticut, Janet Rawlings moved to the U.K. in 1979, a year after graduation. She has lived in Chepstow for the past twelve years and is actively involved with Friends of the Earth.

'When the group was founded here a year and a half ago I resolutely refused to be chairman, but then felt guilty and volunteered to be the recycling campaigner. I've been doing that for the past eighteen, nineteen months. I've got to know a bit about local government and its workings and non-workings and recycling in this area. Other interests have tended to revolve around the children; I'm currently chairman of the PTA at the primary school where two of them go, and on the PTA for the comprehensive school where the eldest one is now.

'I like Chepstow; it's the size of town I like. I grew up really in the suburbs of New York City and I'm not a city person. Chepstow is more the right size. You can get to know most of the people, a lot of people and feel part of the community here. I also like the U.K. in general because the towns grew up – most of them – before the age of the car so they tend to have a small core. You can walk to do most of your shopping, whereas where I grew up you had to drive everywhere, from one shopping centre to the next. So I like British towns in general for that and I've found the British people friendly. And Chepstow in particular; I mean, it is a lovely part of the country. You've got countryside right on the doorstep and it's accessible to London and Heathrow Airport where mothers and things fly in from. We've been happy here in Chepstow.'

Are you conscious of Wales being distinct from England?

'Well, yes, there are all the road signs in two languages. I've enjoyed that. I like learning about places and learning enough Welsh to decipher their roadsigns and placenames that's been enjoyable. Within the last four years the kids – you know, with the National Curriculum – the kids have had to start learning

Welsh a little bit at school. So from that point of view it seems distinct. And now, getting involved with the recycling, I'm realising that the government bureaucracy is separate as well – the Welsh Office and all of that. In a way it seems funny that a country that's been united for so long is still struggling to preserve differences, that there is still a Plaid Cymru that is, you know, trying to push for a bit of independence and would like to be more like Scotland. Being an outsider it's fun to look at the politics and people's attitudes. I've really enjoyed watching American politics and issues reported on the British news over the years. You get a much different slant on things than you do when you live inside the country, especially a country as big and insular as the United States. I mean, you can't change foreign money inside the US because they don't believe there *is* anything besides the US dollar. Where here Britain is part of a larger Europe and realises that.

'My husband gets all upset that forms are put in two languages. I don't think that's bad; I think the Welsh culture should be preserved and maintained, but I don't think political autonomy is at all sensible. There are some Welsh people who would still like that.

'I think Thatcher was good for this country. I think that Labour . . . the pendulum had swung too far towards Labour and labour unions thought they could dictate everything. But I think that privatisation has gone too far now.'

The Labour Party is talking of the possibility of elected Welsh and Scottish assemblies . . .

'Really?'

Do you remember the referendum in 1979?

'No. I came over in '79. I came with Thatcher!'

If Labour were to create such an assembly in Wales, do you think that your work with Friends of the Earth could be done more effectively?

'No, I don't think so. I think things are so integrated in the UK that I don't think that would make any difference. What I *do* think is that it's criminal the way the national government – the Tory Government – is drawing power away from local representatives – representative officials – and centralising it so much in central government. It really doesn't matter what platform county and borough councillors run on because it's up to the central government what money they have to actually spend on local services. They could be all in favour of recycling, the way Cardiff is, but if the Welsh Office says they're going to cap them if they add one penny to the rates to cover expanding kerbside collection schemes there's nothing they can do. They have to give up their policy of bringing kerbside collection to the whole city. I suppose a national assembly would depend on how much autonomy that were given. But I think really all that has to happen is that central government gives back that freedom for local people to elect the local government they want.'

Marian Rees, Tal-y-llyn, Gwynedd*

We are speaking at the house attached to the Post Office in Carno where Marian Rees, fifty-six, is visiting a childhood friend. A native of Llanbrynmair, she has worked for the Welsh Office, the Urdd (Welsh League of Youth), has taught, done Voluntary Service Overseas and has taken early retirement. She is currently engaged in a campaign against the establishment of wind farms in rural Wales.

'I'm against them because they're an example of deceit. Everybody thinks that wind farms produce green energy, clean energy. That isn't true because they bring their own pollution with them. They create a great deal of visual pollution because you have to make large, strong roads up to the mountain tops to put them in place and then you have to pour ton upon ton of concrete into the tops of the mountains to hold them because they can be a hundred, even two hundred feet high. You then have to build roads between them and lay a cable to carry the energy down and create a power station somewhere to receive it and to connect it to the National Grid. So it's something which *visually* is very damaging to the countryside. Also, of course, from the point of view of noise, they create a lot of noise and it's a very unpleasant background noise. People who come to the countryside, or who live there, are there very often because of the peace and quiet. That's destroyed. All this happens and how much profit, who makes the profit . . . why does it happen? If it's so obvious that it is something that pollutes the countryside, why then are people in favour of it? Well, they're being deceived. People say, "Well, it's green energy", but it's not, "and it's cheap energy", they say, but it's not cheap either; it's very expensive. For example, they want to put up sixty of them here now in Mid Wales. It's going to cost almost fifty million. It could cost more because they'll need to put lots and lots and lots of stones and so on on the mountain to create a road because the mountain is basically *peat* and to create a road there will be very, very costly. Also, in order to get big international companies – because they're the people who *build* these wind farms, they're big projects – in order to attract those to build wind farms, the Government gives very extensive grants. They give them a grant of fifty per cent for materials and the cost of construction and then they pay *eleven* pence a unit for every unit of electricity they produce while they only pay *three* pence for electricity which is produced in any other way. So in order to make them attractive they pay people to come here to do the work, they pay people to come here and pollute the countryside. And we're the people who pay for it because there's ten per cent on your electricity bill and mine every time, every quarter, and that goes straight in to pay for non-fossil fuel generation, i.e. atomic and wind.

'People say then, "Well, it's better than atomic". The point is, it doesn't compete with atomic because both are non-fossil fuels and they get exactly the same level of grant from the Government. The Government hasn't got any programme at all for closing down any atomic power station. No matter how many windmills they build they're still going to put up atomic stations. For the simple reason that they produce lots of electricity and these windmills produce next to nothing. As I said, sixty of them are going to provide *light* for twenty-three thousand houses in Newtown. And what's that? It's nothing. So the whole thing's a con because the Government signed in Rio that they were going to do something by the end of the century to reduce the pollution that we put into the air from coal and oil-fired power stations. Well, of course that needed to be done, but they've jumped into this and they've said, "What can I do? Quick, quick, quick. What can I do? What can I do? Something visible, something that people can see. Right, we'll go up to the tops of the mountains, put up a load of windmills and everybody will think we're great." And of course local farmers, they get something out of it, those whose land is used. They get about fifteen hundred or perhaps two thousand for every pylon on their land. But nobody else gets anything, they don't create any jobs. The pylons aren't made locally, it's people from Denmark and Japan who come here to erect them and it's foreign business and the Stock Market in London who own the companies. Nothing comes through to the community from them at all apart from a little money for the occasional farmer to change his Daihatsu every six months. That's all that comes into the local community. And of course the farmers who very often are going to profit financially are the ones who pass the planning. Every District Council is a planning authority and they, of course, can do what they like and so they haven't seen fit to stand up and say, "No we don't want these things; they're going to *ruin* Mid Wales" – for tourism and even for farming, because only some farmers stand to gain, others won't. What they are doing is destroying their own country and the next generation will never ever *ever* forgive them for destroying the character, personality and spirit of the mountains. It'll never come back after tons of concrete are poured into them. Never ever.

'So it's all one big . . . the whole thing's a big con-trick and it's high time the nation stood up and said, "Thus far and no further". They've taken the water; they've taken the coal; they've taken over farming through the European grants system – the farmer can't move an inch without their saying yea or nay. And the last thing we have left is the beauty, the beauty of Wales. Beauty is the only natural asset we have left in Wales and ask any foreigners who come here – any Frenchman or German or anyone on holiday – what do they think of Wales, "Oh, it's so *beautiful,* it's so natural". But we're selling all that, you know, down the river.

'Even in Montgomeryshire itself there are twenty other plans in the pipeline now. Another twenty. Mid Wales is being especially targeted for the reason that this is the soft underbelly. It's not protected. It's not a National Park; it's not an Area of Outstanding Natural Beauty on the map – but it is; and it's precious and there's remoteness here. It's an area that's not been covered with roads; it's a difficult area to reach and that's a very rare thing in Wales today. And that's the sort of thing they're selling for nothing to . . . well, to this completely inhuman Government we have at present, which wants to turn everything into money.'

How do you view the future of rural Wales?

'My opinion of farming is that it isn't farming any more. I think that farmers have been too much influenced by the Ministry of Agriculture, to such an extent that they've become a sort of monoculture. They don't use the farm in its totality any more; they don't farm anything but sheep, or sometimes sheep and cattle. They don't even grow potatoes. I'm the only one in Tal-y-llyn who digs up a potato in the garden. Nobody now makes anything out of the land; they don't produce anything for the table; they don't even kill their own meat – they buy it back from the butcher; they don't keep chickens or turkeys or geese or guinea fowl or any of the things they used to keep in the past; they don't keep a pig; they don't keep a cow for milking; they don't try to make butter or cheese and farm kitchens now are like some kitchen in suburbia, all formica and ceramic tiles and completely characterless. The food in the fridge is exactly the same food you'd find in suburbia, things bought from Kwiks and LoCost and Safeway and ready-cooked and carried to the farm. The thing's disgraceful, I think. Our way of life, the old healthy, complete, interesting way of life has been totally eroded and people have been mesmerised by shops like Iceland where they go and buy their prepacked food. They're poisoning themselves. And I say, in half a century there'll be a big change with people in the towns turning round and saying, "Hey, we don't want to buy food packaged like this, which has been produced in these big factory farms. We want it labelled, we want to know exactly where it's come from and we want to know that it's been produced in a way that's as organic and painless as possible. And we're not going to eat it unless we know that". And I hope that that revolution will happen. We need the Welsh farm-cum-smallholding back again in all its glory and we need a local market selling all this food; we need to kill the animals locally and we need a local butcher labelling the meat so that we know *precisely* where it's come from, so we have a choice. We've got no choice any more. We talk about this country as a free country, there's no choice here at all.'

John Roberts, Brecon, Powys*

John Roberts is a small, neat man in a large, busy room, the Brecon and Radnor county office of the Farmers' Union of Wales. He comes from generations of Carmarthenshire farming stock and was born on a mixed farm. He has held his present post for the last eight years and during that time has seen the number of staff grow from two to five. He speaks here in a personal capacity.

'We're going through a period of change in agriculture. There have been momentous events over the last decade and there are certain to be more before the turn of the century. Over the last twenty years we've seen a number of small family farms disappear and large units take their place. Having said that, we're also seeing now the medium-sized units going too . . . but I suppose that the biggest burden at the moment which is weighing farmers down is the amount of forms they have to cope with and that's where my job comes in offering help to our members . . . practical help to fill in forms and advising them in various ways as far as planning goes on hundreds of matters.

'Quotas remains a big issue because of the categorisation of those who can make an application for an extra quota. To tell you the truth, it causes dreadful worry to many of our young people who are trying to make a start in agriculture. We have one example – and to be honest there are lots of examples in this area – where this has taken place and it's received publicity recently, especially around the time of the Royal Welsh Show, where there's a young married couple with over a thousand sheep and a quota for only thirteen. So it creates a huge problem. Perhaps they have a bank that's been kind to them thus far but that's not going to last and perhaps before the end of the year they'll be out of business. The rationale behind a quota, of course, is over-production. Wales and Great Britain don't tend to over-produce, but because we're part of a larger unit – namely Europe – and over-production happens there, it squeezes Welsh agriculture too.'

Does the FUW campaign for Wales to be considered separately?

Yes, but because some of the circumstances of Welsh farmers are totally different to those of farmers in England. Take for example the difference that exists as far as grain goes. The payments they get in England are a fair bit more than they get in Wales. The excuse is that we don't produce as much to the acre, or hectare as it is now. Now, the facts have been put together by a new group which has sprung up because of this injustice, that we produce as much if not more than producers across the border. So the whole thing is unfair to Wales. We've seen this as far as other payments go, too. Take for example the ESAs – Environmentally Sensitive Areas. As far as payments per hectare go they get more in corresponding areas in England than they do in Wales. So again there's an injustice.'

Does farming within a National Park pose problems?

'This is a big issue in Brecon and Radnor. Farmers within the Brecon Beacons National Park feel that they're . . . second-rate people. There are restrictions on them with regard to planning; there are restrictions with regard to farming. If they were to receive more money because of that everything would be OK, but that doesn't happen. In the Park that we have here – and I say this without a moment's hesitation – the money's channelled to the Park itself. The biggest growth area within the Brecon Beacons National Park is staff. Also, they own more land than any other Park and so the money doesn't go where it's due, that is, to the farmers, the people who really look after the countryside. It's come to the point where the Councils who contribute financially are looking and saying "Hey, we're not going to do it," and we've seen where Mid Glamorgan has refused to contribute this year. So the Park's got financial problems and they've got to look at changing direction. Perhaps the answer is that we have – and there's been talk about it already – a one-stop shop where everybody goes for finance for conservation. Everyone will go to the same source. Perhaps jobs will be lost, but there'll be more money available for the people who need it.

'I can't afford to be pessimistic. Farming has *always* been a part of the life of Wales, and it *must* continue. Farming is what conserves the countryside best and it must continue otherwise who knows what will happen to our countryside. We must in the future look for ways so that our young people have an opportunity to come into farming. We also need to be looking at the way in which the Welsh Office does its job – there's been an overflow of forms. I'm heartened by the determination of young people. For example, we saw it during last year when two County Council units had come up for lease: one small farm – about thirty acres – and one about sixty. And with the sixty acre one, over sixty young farmers applied to become tenant to the County Council. So there are people deciding to farm still . . . We've got to sit down, talk to each other, co-operate with each other. No, I can't be pessimistic about the future.'

O.M. Roberts, Llanbedrycennin, Conwy, Gwynedd*

O.M. Roberts is eighty-eight, an articulate and fascinating man, who has lived a full public life as a J.P., member of Gwynedd County Council and the Welsh Joint Education Committee. He joined the Welsh Nationalist Party, the forerunner to Plaid Cymru, as a student in 1926, a year after its inception. For over fifty years he kept secret his involvement in the Bombing School arson attack of 1936 at Penyberth, Llŷn, a milestone in nationalist history. Apart from a year's teaching in London, he has lived his whole life in Caernarfonshire, although his present home in the Conwy Valley is different in many respects from his roots in the quarrying villages of Llanrug and Llanddeiniolen.

'I remember going to a meeting in Caernarfon in November 1926 where Dyfnallt [Rev. J. Dyfnallt Owen, a founder member of the Welsh Nationalist Party] was speaking with Robert Williams Parry [the poet and lecturer] in the chair. In that meeting two of my friends joined. I took a membership form back to Bangor with me and said that I'd think the thing over. I completed it and sent it back a day or two later. Now, at the College in Bangor there was the 'Three-Gs', *Y Gymdeithas Genedlaethol Gymreig* [Welsh Nationalist Society]. It had in fact been a political society, concerned with Irish ideas on nationalism, and as a result had been very unpopular in the College. Well, when I arrived at Bangor in 1925 I became a member. It had stopped being so – how can I put it? – militaristic, by then. Well, H.R. Jones, the national organiser for Plaid came along to one of the meetings to try and persuade us to form a branch of the Party in College, and that's what happened. So from 1926 on Bangor had its own branch of the Welsh Nationalist Party.

'In 1929 Plaid fought its first General Election seat. I was at the meeting in the Pendref hotel, Caernarfon, where Lewis Valentine was adopted as candidate. A giant of a man, physically and spiritually. I don't apologise for saying this: I think that the fact that Plaid fought the seat made a huge difference to politics in Wales. Certainly, the amount of attention given to Wales at the time was minimal. I don't think that Wales and the Welsh language would have been paid any attention politically unless the Welsh Nationalist Party had pricked the conscience of the other parties. We polled 609 votes, but it was the start, a very feeble start but a very important one, I think.'

And Plaid Cymru in recent years?

'I must say that I think that it's lost its vision. It never seemed to me that Dafydd Wigley or Dafydd Elis Thomas had the fire in the belly that Gwynfor [Evans] had. It has tried to make itself popular. Look at the south Wales Valleys especially. We try to influence them to join Plaid Cymru and end up steering policy in such a way as to make it acceptable and that doesn't pay in my opinion. I'm one of those people who believe that what does pay is to speak the truth and convince people. And the fact is that membership in the Valleys hasn't increased despite the fact that Dafydd [Elis Thomas] has tried to please them.'

What hope do you see for the future?

'One of the things that cheers me greatly is the consistent and fervent demand for Welsh-medium schools in the anglicised areas of the south. It doesn't follow that this will translate itself into a political interest, but it makes me hopeful that there will be Welsh speakers there who know a little about Welsh history, something – and I'm sorry to say this – that the socialists of the Valleys don't know. Or at least they didn't. Perhaps things are different now.'

David Senior, Newtown, Powys

An unexpected meeting on a Sunday afternoon. David Senior is busy reading through National Curriculum Key Stage 2 Science documents in a terraced house near the centre of Newtown. It is sparsely furnished, with pastel orange walls. The only decorations are a large Red Dragon flag and a sign balanced on the mantelpiece announcing it to be the regional offices of Plaid Cymru the Welsh Nationalist Party. David is thirty, born in Newtown and raised in Forden. He has been a member of Plaid for seven years.

'I joined Plaid Cymru because I went to university in Kent and noticed levels of ignorance, if you like. Not maliciousness; I don't think that there's anything anti-Welsh in most English people, it's a level of ignorance. Came back, was a builder here for about seven years, self-employed builder – small, I think at the most I was employing four, five people at any one time. Then the depression came; building became very, very unpleasant; a reasonable amount of work if you were prepared not to make any money, which obviously isn't very pleasant, so I went back to college, retrained as a teacher and I'm starting my first full-time teaching job in September, just over the border in Shropshire.

'Plaid is surprisingly active locally. A small band of people very active on a wide range of issues. Unfortunately we don't tend to get a great deal of publicity or anything. I think that's probably true for the Labour Party in the area as well. The local paper is more or less non-political, therefore the remarks of the MP get reported and the remarks of the Chairman of the Mid Wales Development get reported and so on. If you're in a *position* you get reported; if you're not in an official position then you don't on the whole. So however active you are it doesn't tend to make a huge impression on the people of the area, which obviously makes life quite hard – hard work. We've got *quite* a strong membership. Oddly enough, the bulk of the activity comes from the English-speaking east of the constituency and the bulk of the membership comes from the Welsh-speaking west of the constituency. I think that's perhaps because a lot of

Welsh speakers tend to join who aren't political. They're not political, but they do have an allegiance to Wales, an allegiance to their culture, so they want to support but they don't want to get involved in "politics". We do quite well in certain contexts in the area; we've got several councillors who are independents on the District Council and openly Plaid Cymru but not officially Plaid Cymru councillors – which, of course, is a source of irritation to the Party, but also a good way of getting things done. So it's a two-edged sword.'

How do you regard the Party nationally?

'I don't like Plaid Cymru national conferences any more. We now have a system whereby all the branches get to vote on the motions that they would like to see brought to Conference. This means nothing very controversial ever gets there, because whilst it may have the virulent support of half the branches, it's going to need more than the support of half the branches to get it on the agenda. Up until quite recently Plaid Cymru national conferences tended to be quite good debates. These were often portrayed on TV as everyone trying to plunge a dagger into everyone else's back and the split-up of the Party and everything else. So there's been a response – which I think has taken place in most political parties – to try to turn the conference into something more of a shop window for the party, and to have the actual real debate taking place away from the media. It does mean now that at Conference we'll be discussing the language – again. We'll be discussing a campaign for devolution in Wales – again. Which are all things which we tend to know what we think about anyway. There will probably be quite a major debate on . . . health, I would have thought that would be one of the more controversial debates there. But I don't see anything very controversial getting through the Conference.'

What would you like to see on the agenda?

' . . . I'd like to see Plaid Cymru take a more internationalist view than it does. The conferences can be a bit parochial, which again . . . this is, if you have a vote amongst all the branches then the more immediate issues tend to get discussed. I think we should be taking a view on what is happening in Bosnia, what is happening in other areas of the world where you've got a similar situation: one group of people wanting to run their own affairs and another group *not* wanting them to run their own affairs. I think that Plaid Cymru could actually contribute to that debate in a way that doesn't happen at the present. The international view is created by the national governments, and all of the national governments tend to take a similar point of view when it comes to anyone wanting to break away from a country. So I'd like to see us start actually debating issues like that and moving out into areas that aren't quite so definitely purely Welsh. The upper part of the Party – the MPs and the National Executive – are quite internationalist from that point of view, but I think the bulk of the membership perhaps isn't. So very often there isn't a party view. I don't think there's a party view on Bosnia. There's probably a general sympathy in favour of the Muslims, but there's no official view and no worked-out policy or anything in those terms.'

What difference would a Plaid programme make to the state of Wales, if implemented?

'I think the influence of most political parties is surprisingly little. The state of Wales is quite good at present, I think. To be fair, a lot of the claims that the Government make about Wales doing quite well are true. I think that's probably got very little to do with the Government in actual fact. We have done quite well in recent years. I suspect we'd have probably done quite well under Labour or Plaid or whatever. There are certain things . . . because of the Government we've got, Wales has got the same problems, largely, as the rest of Britain. If you're one of the more unfortunate in society then you are not going to be helped as much as you would have been under a different government and I *think* that can cause a certain amount of conflict. And I think this will tend to benefit Plaid Cymru; quite possibly because, when you're looking for somebody to blame, you quite often look for a distant government which is in another area of the country, you look at other ethnic groups, you look at other social groups and you vote for something that opposes them. It could mean that Plaid Cymru will gain votes from people it would rather not gain votes from, who are just looking for somebody to blame for their problems. I think if Plaid Cymru were to, if you like, gain independence for Wales and then govern the country, I think the *main* change would actually be in terms of the amount of care taken of people who are less fortunate within society. There would be a greater emphasis on making sure that people had a minimum level of housing, a minimum level of health care and so on. And so in fact it might not be hugely different from what we might find if we get a Labour government in Britain as a whole. But I think if Wales was to gain independence what would happen is that people in Wales would have to take responsibility for themselves. They wouldn't have somebody else to blame, they wouldn't have somebody else to pick on and say it's *their* fault that we're poor, it's *their* fault that we're homeless. It would be *Wales's* fault if people in Wales were homeless and it would be up to Wales to actually deal with those problems. It's quite comfortable to be part of Britain because you can always blame the English. London government, they're to blame, you know, and it means that we can actually sit back and feel quite smug. If we become independent, it will be down to us.'

Annette Shaw, Llanrug, and Dafydd Lloyd, Caernarfon, Gwynedd

A couple on a train thundering through Deeside. Annette has lived in the Caernarfon area 'on and off' for the past twenty years. Born into a working class background in Birmingham, she now speaks with the placeless accent of a woman used to travelling. She is divorced, with two grown sons. Dafydd's accent is unmistakably north Walian. He was born in Beddgelert, of mixed Irish-Welsh parentage and is a fluent Welsh speaker. They are both in their late forties. Dafydd speaks first.

'I've travelled the best part of the world as an engineer in petrochemicals and a chef, but I've always maintained a home in Wales. I started to travel once I could walk; I was hungry to travel. I drifted to London in the mid-sixties and I've been commuting back and forth ever since – definitely for the past twenty-two years. It was a group of us originally. It started as jolly and now it's a matter of survival. There's just no way I can maintain any sort of professional livelihood in Wales. I worked for a bit in the Welsh film industry, but it's totally stitched up by the Taffia. They don't want anybody to have to share their slice of the cake with.'

Your time away from Wales has coincided not only with the expansion of Welsh media, but also a surge in electoral support for nationalism, especially in Gwynedd. Do you notice any change in the political climate?

'I wasn't aware of any anti-Englishness until I was in my mid-twenties, but you can't get away from it now. When I was growing up no-one seemed to be politically aware, but it's young people now who seem to be carrying the anti-English banner. I've got two kids, a son nineteen and a daughter sixteen, educated in Penygroes, and to be honest they have great difficulty speaking English.'

Are you at all political?

'I'm apolitical to lost sodding causes! For me at the moment it's all about economic self-survival.'

Annette is more sanguine:

'I'm part of an English clique, what you could call a sub-culture of one-parent families up in the hills. It's an easy, comfortable environment to live in. You know, a healthy lifestyle for the children, mountaineering, canoeing and all that sort of stuff. But Dafydd's dead right . . . the biggest problem here is the language. There were a lot of English-Welsh problems when the kids reached secondary school – bullying and so on. It didn't seem to happen at primary school, or at least I wasn't aware of it. As a sort of defence mechanism, my two developed a real work ethic. It was part survival and part taking advantage of the system. They were quite academic and it's easy to be a big fish. They're achievers. The youngest is a film-maker with MTV in London and the other manages a printing business – a very successful one – in Cheshire. My own background wasn't one of great achievement. I went into adult ed. and ended up lecturing for a while at a Tech, YTS, Basic Skills, Tom Sharpe *Wilt* stuff.

'Wales is a great place for doing nothing in. When I need to work I tend to work away. I worked with Monty Python in London for three years and did catering in Holland between 1991 and 92. I don't suppose I have much of a social life here. Ours is a very Welsh street; I've got great neighbours, but not many Welsh friends as such. The Welsh intelligentsia can be a pain, but I tend to be relaxed about it and not let them use me as a scapegoat. You know, all the time my kids were growing up here, they were never addressed in Welsh. My mum and dad have retired here now, and my dad learned Welsh to fit in. He hasn't, and he thinks it's a cultural thing. Fluency's no problem, he says, but not being a Welshman is.

'If I had the chance, I'd go abroad again, but not England. I like the pace of life here, the environment.'

Dafydd half agrees.

Cathy Shea, Cardiff

Cathy Shea is thirty-one and secretary of Cardiff City Supporters' Club. She comes from a working-class background in Whitchurch, the youngest but one of six children, and still lives in the area.

'I first got into football around the season 1974-75, when I was about thirteen – when my brother used to tolerate my going to games with him. My first game ever was the heady heights of watching Cardiff versus Chesterfield. At the time I don't think I even knew where Chesterfield was. Since then I've probably been there on about four occasions. But he soon realised that I really enjoyed the game. I learned about the game and basically I love it.'

Since then, what game have you enjoyed the most?

'The most outstanding thing I can think of is Cardiff winning the Third Division Championship at Scunthorpe in May 1993 – which had been a very long, hard season. But seeing four thousand Cardiff fans behaving and enjoying themselves at a game . . . well, it was enjoyable and it was probably the only game I enjoyed the whole season as a spectacle. With Wales, the major game would be the game with Romania at the National Stadium. A packed crowd, all we needed to do was win and we were going to the World Cup, we were safe. And the crowd, it was charged, it was electric, there were hand-flares, people sang all the way through. But unfortunately a missed penalty and a bit of bad luck and once again Wales were the nearly-men of British football. Of course that was all tinged with sadness because of an incident with a marine flare which caused the death of a football fan, which is something that should never ever happen at football. Football is a family game; you feel that you ought to be able to take your family and sit in peace and quiet.

'I travel everywhere with Cardiff City. I'm hoping to travel away with Wales now with the European Championships. I enjoy it. I've got a nice circle of friends, a lot of women, families

. . . and I think football is on the up in Wales. I'm trying to take in all ninety-two grounds. It's just nice to be accepted away from home, to meet other people, to talk about their likes and dislikes in football. Everybody's the same; they're just wearing a different colour shirt.

'The biggest influence on me in football would have to be my brother. He took me to my first away game, away at Bristol Rovers the year we got promoted in 82-83. Actually I think he's now quite proud of my association with Cardiff City Football Club and Cardiff City Supporters' Club itself. I actually played ladies' league football for nine years, which gave me the passion for the sport, I think. Anybody that can travel to places like Truro from Cardiff on a Sunday morning at seven o'clock must love the sport very dearly. But I gave up playing to be able to get more involved with Cardiff City . . . I think there are more women going, definitely. There are certainly more single females joining the Supporters' Club, and it is a love of the *sport* rather than any other involvement! The Supporters' Club has had about a three hundred per cent rise in family membership over the past three years. You walk through Cardiff and you see more Cardiff City football shirts than rugby shirts, which you wouldn't have seen a few years ago. It's a nice thought that at some stage you're going to have all-seater stadiums packed with families, enjoying the People's Game without a hint of trouble. A nice thought.'

Chris Simpson, Aberystwyth, Dyfed

Born in Leeds, Dr Chris Simpson has worked as a consultant pathologist at Bronglais Hospital since 1982. He is married with three daughters, is a town councillor for the Green Party locally and a Welsh learner. He has been interested in green politics since 1979. At the 1992 General Election, Ceredigion elected Cynog Dafis to Parliament under a Plaid Cymru /Green banner.

'We've got a house within a mile of the hospital, and that's quite deliberate, so I can just walk to work. Aberystwyth is a very nice-sized town. It's a town on a human scale, I always think, in that you can walk or cycle everywhere. You don't have to worry about getting the last bus home or anything like that.

'The Ceredigion local party is the largest and most active in Wales. We actually have between twenty and twenty-five per cent of the total membership. And of course we were very closely involved in getting Cynog Dafis elected, which we think was a great idea. We think Cynog is doing really well, but unfortunately there has been something of a split, like there was with *Die Grunen* in Germany, between the *realos* [realists] and the *fundies* [fundamentalists]. We're on the *realo* side, if you like. We want to co-operate with people and get their green agenda going. And there are lots of people in Wales on the fundamentalist side who want to be pure green and get *that* going. So there's been a big division in the Green Party in Wales for the last three or four years over this question. It's come to prominence particularly because of the fact that in Ceredigion we've been co-operating with Plaid Cymru. Part of the problem is that Plaid Cymru have an image problem in other parts of Wales such as South Glam. And so Green Party members don't wanted to be tainted, if you like, with this image of co-operation with Plaid Cymru.

'We only got into this co-operation because Plaid have moved so much towards the Green position. And it just happens in Ceredigion that a lot of the active members of Plaid Cymru were very green-thinking in their perspective. I accept that in other parts of Wales Plaid Cymru are not necessarily so green, but as a

Green Party member I prefer to work with them and draw them more towards the green position than to stand away from them and say, "I not going to touch you with a barge-pole because you're not one hundred per cent green." That's just the way I look at things. In Ceredigion members of both parties have gained from co-operation. It's not a one way street by any means, though people outside might have the opinion – which would be wrong – of Plaid Cymru just wanting to take us along just so they could get Cynog in. It wasn't like that at all.

'Originally we wanted to have a joint candidate, but there were constitutional problems for both parties and problems with the electoral system in Westminster. So, basically, he's "Plaid Cymru – Gwyrddion/Green". Those were the four words. Not Green Party, just Green. So he was Plaid Cymru with the backing of the Green Party.'

What are the prospects for similar co-operation elsewhere? In Carmarthen, for instance?

'That really would depend on the members in the area because the Green Party is a very decentralist party. It just happened in Ceredigion that we had ninety per cent support so we had a mandate to go ahead with it. With something as out of the ordinary as this, you'd have to have a large majority of the members in favour.'

Does green politics have a specifically Welsh dimension?

'We always stress devolution and local activity. Not counting the English immigrants, in the context of Ceredigion there tends to be a very settled population. The Welsh tend to be settled, with a well-developed sense of identity and belongingness. And that all fits in with green politics. What I'd like to see is the development of local economies, because one of the answers to the unemployment problem is to get people working locally to produce the things they need themselves. And if in the future we happen to have a Green government that would be one of the ideas to get the economy going again. If you look over the period of a hundred, two hundred years, you can see how all the little local economies have gradually been subsumed into one large economy and that's being subsumed into a global economy. So you get the idiocy of truckloads of stuff being ferried hundreds of miles when it could all be done locally anyway. And then you wouldn't have the problem of road transport and pollution ands so on and so on. It's areas like Wales, and other areas in Europe that are similar where green politics and local economies take root. And that would be the example for places like urban England where it doesn't yet apply in the same context. Green politics could well take off in Wales because of the advantages of the Welsh context.

'A lot of the Welsh-speaking community see the Green Party as a party for the English immigrants in Wales and not the party for them. But although I'm an English immigrant I don't see it that way at all. I think that green politics and the Green Party has a lot to offer Welsh people.'

Mair Spencer, Clocaenog, Clwyd*

Canolfan Iaith Clwyd *occupies a suite of rooms on a corner site in Denbigh. It was opened in 1991, working in partnership with local colleges and the WEA 'to ensure the best possible service for Welsh learners in Clwyd'. Mair Spencer is employed as Tutor Organiser. She is forty-eight, a native of Nefyn, Llŷn, and speaks in the slightly deliberate Welsh of someone used to conversing with learners. We talk in an empty classroom.*

'I wasn't Tutor Organiser at the time, but when this centre opened it was a dream come true for everybody to come together in one place. I remember when we wanted the place to be ready for classes to start in the September and the learners and me and the children and everyone painting. Everybody was socialising, everybody painting, cleaning the toilets, everything. It didn't matter what work we did, everybody was one together. And that's what's good when learners come in. You know, there are some on the dole, there are others who are doctors, but everybody mixes. Nobody's cleverer than anybody else, everybody's at the same level when they're learning a language, and I like that a lot.

'Classes start in the morning at half past nine. Some go on till half past twelve. Perhaps we'll have three different classes, say three different levels, at the same time. So the working day starts, to tell the truth, at nine in the morning and finishes at ten at night . . . because I'm so fond of my work, you know, I work in the evenings too. A lot of the learners become personal friends. You know, you grow very, very close to them and all the hours they put in, *Dew*, they deserve a lot of credit.

'We've got a nursery here for the very small children. Perhaps some of the fathers are out of work and the mothers are working, so they can come here for Welsh classes. So we've got a little nursery here, like a crèche. Also, of course, we do GCSE and A Level examinations and we've had very good results, delightful this year. They've worked so hard. Some come here and have extra private lessons every Wednesday afternoon. We've got a Welsh club here and they pay £2 a year to join and then we have different activities, different people coming here to speak and *Merched y Wawr* also come in to help, you know, to talk to them, so that's very popular.'

I noticed posters in French, Breton and German on the walls. Is that part of the Centre's work?

'That's right. Christine Berry – she's a girl from Brittany and she's married a Welshman, Dyfrig Berry from Denbigh here – and she comes here. Of course Christine's completely fluent in Welsh. I can't imagine her speaking any other language to tell you the truth. Christine comes here. She holds French lessons, through the medium of Welsh of course – everything we do here is through the medium of Welsh – and she has a Breton class, too. Then there's a lady here who's lived in Mexico and she comes in to teach Spanish through the medium of Welsh, and Peter Smith, who's also learned Welsh, who comes here to give German lessons through the medium of Welsh.'

How do you see the development of teaching Welsh as a second language?

'I'm sure it's improved from year to year. There are more resources now. We've got videos now. I remember when I started and, say, I had twenty-one in the class, if I'd prepare work at home, well it would take all day to write out twenty-one sheets of A4, but I had to do it. But now of course our biggest friend, Elsi the photocopier, when she's working . . . that's been a big help to me.'

Are teaching methods more sophisticated?

'Well . . . perhaps to an extent. I'm not sure. I tend to teach in the same way as I was trained to teach. Remember there's a lot of stuff available, but I'd say that we need more still. I'd like to see more pictures, more language games and such. I like to do all my evening class work over the weekend and it's hard because I work a lot of Saturdays. So I've only got Sunday and

I've got a family – I've got five children and a husband and somebody's got to clean the house and do the washing! So I'd like to see more things like homework already written rather than having to do it myself. Perhaps I'd still prepare what I want to do myself, perhaps I'd still do that, but I'd like it if there were things available for me to make quick copies. But I'm not complaining. Everything's great, to be honest.'

How much contribution have your Welsh learners made to Welsh life in Wales?

'To tell the truth, these learners, lots of them do more than natural Welsh speakers, those who've learned fluently. I can name lots of people. I've got some who've been in my class, they're on Glyndŵr Council. They stand for Plaid and different other parties. There's one running a Welsh-medium nursery, there's others who've joined *Merched y Wawr*. And we've got one here, David Ball, who's learning and he's just been on a long-distance walk over the mountains from Prestatyn to Neath to the National Eisteddfod and he and his wife spent twelve days walking in order to collect money for the Centre. How many Welsh would be prepared to do that? I'd be prepared to do other things, but not sleeping in a tent in the middle of nowhere, you know.

'I don't know if you remember the time when we wanted S4C? Well, I very nearly went to prison for the language. I wanted a Welsh channel for the sake of my children and I was in court here in Denbigh and lots of learners came to support me and I'm extremely proud that I was able to do that for my country and I'm thrilled that S4C has been so successful. At the time I had five little girls, the eldest was eight and the youngest seven months old and I was prepared to go to prison. I had seven days to pay the fine or I'd have been in for two months and I was determined that I wasn't going to pay. The very last thing I wanted to do was leave all my children. I didn't want to go to prison and leave them all at home, I had no mother myself to look after them. I had a good husband, but he couldn't . . . you know, he had to go to work too. In the end friends collected money for me. And when I went to the court here, one thing I do remember. There was no Welsh Bible to swear your oath on. And of course I'd been to a Welsh Sunday school, Welsh chapel and I'd never before in my life read an English Bible. And when they opened the English Bible in front of me, I thought, Oh . . . I didn't want to show off, because I'm not that religious. I like to pray on my own and so on. I go to chapel, but not three times on a Sunday . . . but I said to myself, I *can't* put my hands on this English Bible. It's not my language, not my language. Anyway I went out and I bought a Welsh Bible for the court in Denbigh. And I'm pleased that I did that, not to get publicity for myself, but because I thought it was very important to have a Welsh Bible in a court in Denbigh. And what they said was, "Oh, somebody must have pinched the Welsh one." I asked them, "May I have a Welsh Bible, please?" to put my hand on, and they said, "Somebody must have pinched the Welsh one". That's what I got. Never mind. I went to Siop Clwyd and I got one, as a present for them. So I'm very proud that I've been able to do that much for Wales, for my children's sake, for their children in the future, I hope, and for other people. And all the learners, you know, are pleased with S4C. Of course I say, "Remember to watch television and tell me what you've heard this week." And they come back and say . . . sometimes they've understood very little, some of them understand hardly anything, a few words, but thanks be for S4C – and *Radio Cymru* of course.'

Helen Strigner, Abergele, Clwyd

Helen Strigner was born in Northampton but has lived in Wales since the age of eight. She trained as a nurse in London and followed a course in midwifery in Bristol before marrying and returning to the Llangollen area. For the past two years she has worked as a fundraising and public relations officer for the Clwyd branch of Wales Red Cross, Croes Goch Cymru.

'I needed a job, I saw it in the paper, I have a long experience of voluntary work with scouting and a few other things and I thought that it looked like a challenge. I like working with people.

'How we raise money is a big issue. We do events, but events are very time-consuming if you haven't got lots of volunteers. We do corporate appeals, we look for legacies, we look for general donations, I do lots of public relations, as well, to try and get people to give money. We sell our services . . . we do a lot of first aid at work training and that brings in money, and other public training. We sell the service of first aid cover at events. We do, really, anything that's legal that'll raise money. We do medical loan whereby you lend out wheelchairs and things like that and ask for donations. Then of course there's flag week when you see us on the street, collecting. Collections in shops and that sort of thing.

'And how the money is spent, really, is not at all how people would expect of Red Cross. Most people think of Red Cross as international work, disaster relief and blood and bandages, but here at home, like in all the other regional branches, it's community care. We run clubs for elderly and handicapped people and we run holidays for young people and adults with special needs. We do beauty care, we do hospital trolleys . . . all sorts of things like that, it's all community-based.

How independent are you of the Red Cross nationally?

'Completely. Every branch, that's every county in the U.K., is a charity in its own right. That said, British Red Cross tries to do a universal service. We have a thing called the Five Year Plan, where we're supposed to have core services, which are emergency work, community work, training, youth work – we have a youth section – and what we call tracing welfare, where we try and trace people . . . families who have been separated due to conflict and disaster. Those are the core services and everyone's supposed to provide them, but in Wales, I and my colleagues in the other branches feel very strongly about having a Welsh identity for Red Cross, and in fact we do call ourselves *Croes Goch Cymru* and we are trying to get NHQ to let us produce more and more things in bilingual form. All the directors of the branches meet as the Welsh directors – we're a region, recognised by NHQ as a region – and the other fundraisers and I meet together and try and devise what we're going to do to promote Red Cross as Red Cross Wales. Because we feel very strongly that to a lot of people in Wales a thing like Red Cross looks like an English-imposed thing on Wales, and it isn't meant to be that way. But it's quite obvious that in many parts of Wales there are very few of us who are Welsh speakers – there are *some*. One of my colleagues is a fluent Welsh speaker, I'm a learner and another is a learner. We do our best. We just feel that it's very important. We all have children who go to Welsh schools, or nearly all of us.

'Working for Red Cross is a strange thing to do. It's not an easy message to sell. If you work for something like RSPCA or NSPCC or the Royal Society for the Protection of Birds it's quite obvious to everybody what your message is: you're looking after animals or children or birds, but nobody really knows what Red Cross does. It is a very mixed message and nobody really realises that what we are about is care in the community. Primarily we were set up for emergency post-care and older people in the community will think of us in that way. But it's completely different now.'

Do you sometimes feel that you're doing the work of the statutory agencies?

'Certainly things have changed a lot since the Community Care Act came into being and we do find that we are increasingly being asked to do things perhaps Social Services or the district nurse haven't funds or resources to do. It changes the face of what you do. The Headquarters are encouraging us to look at being more professional and making contracts with local authorities, but there are big pitfalls with that kind of approach. It's difficult to take out contracts if what you're providing is a service with volunteers and it certainly changes the aspect of the branch and it certainly changes the feelings of the volunteers. You can get into difficulties with, "Well, you're being paid for it, but we're not, we're volunteers" and there's a problem about raising enough volunteers to provide a service of the quality you would want to provide. So I think that we all have to go through an exercise of knowing exactly what it is that we want to do, choosing a key project and saying, "Right, these are the ones we want to do. Now we need to raise some volunteers at least specifically for those projects", because it's no good taking on a project if you haven't got the people to do it with and, to my mind and to everybody's mind, the important thing is to provide a *quality* service and not just a very wide-ranging, bits-and-pieces service.'

What projects have been successful?

'We have five centres that have clubs for elderly people. We have one centre in particular, in Old Colwyn, that's a very good community-base centre in that it has a club for elderly people, a club for handicapped people, a club for people who are visually impaired, two playgroups, and there's a cake-decorating club that meets there as well. And it's a real community centre. Then we have the projects for holidays. We take every year about forty or fifty adults with special needs to Pontins at Morecambe with lots of other Red Cross branches for a week's holiday . . . which for most of these people is the only holiday they get, and for most of the carers it's the only break they get. Also every year we take two lots of children with special needs on holiday, a total of about twenty-four, to Pentre-llyn-cymmer, near Cerrigydrudion, the outdoor centre, and they go for about five days with an equal number of our young people and some adult helpers, and they do all sorts of exciting things. It's the same for them – for many of them it's the only break they get and for many of their carers it's the only break they get. So those are extremely worthwhile projects and very, very rewarding to help on and to work with. We all love them, even though they are very hard work. And of course we've got to raise money for those – large amounts of money. The three holiday projects between them cost about £12,000. And that's one of the things I spend time doing, writing away for donations to other organisations like Rotary, the Soroptimists and Lions and nice people like that. There are many and varied other projects. We have several youth groups and quite often they get involved in small, local projects.

'I love Wales. As I say, I've lived here for most of my life and I feel like I'm an adopted Welshwoman. I wouldn't really like to live anywhere else. It's got into my blood, I miss it every time I go away. I love the language even though I can't speak it fluently yet and I feel that there's something extremely special about it. Personally, I've never had any problems with the Welshness business. Some people I know from other parts of Britain say, "Oh well, you go to Wales and everybody breaks out and starts speaking Welsh and you feel isolated". But I don't. I've lived in very small villages where most of what's spoken is in Welsh and it hasn't ever been a problem. I just love it: I love the scenery, I love the hills and I would hate to have to leave Wales.'

Harry Thomas, Prestatyn, Clwyd

Harry Thomas is forty-six. The walls of his flat are covered with pre-War memorabilia, every shelf piled with ancient Oxo tins, cigarette packets and boxes that once held soap. In the hallway stands a row of fairground fruit machines, bagatelles and devices which predict your future. Pride of place, however, goes to a collection of photographs and postcards of old Prestatyn. Harry is acknowledged to be the authority on local history.

'I come from Anglesey and we moved to Gwespyr, five miles outside Prestatyn, in 1950 and my roots are in that village now. I started the hobby of postcard collecting twenty-five years ago when I found myself out of work and it's probably the best thing, the most therapeutic thing, I've ever done in my life, next to having my children. It's snowballed amazingly, postcard-collecting. I travel all over the country collecting old postcards of Prestatyn and I think the need to preserve the history and heritage of where we live is very important and valuable. And one way is by collecting old photographs and preserving them and when we look at them we're looking at views that have vanished for ever: the views showing the High Street and the old shops, the carnival. Over the years I've been commissioned to write four books and I'm working on my fifth one now and I've got a local history page in the local paper. I also present slide-shows in the town each week during the summer season. To me, it's my whole life at the moment.

'There's eighteen thousand people in Prestatyn and, believe it or not, in 1848 when the railway opened in the town and the first holiday-maker started coming in to taste the air and sea-bathe, there were only two hundred and fifty. A lot of the people liked the place so much they came back and made their homes here. With Prestatyn being an important seaside resort at the turn of the century, I'd love to have been alive, I think, wearing a top hat and tails and carrying a cane, walking along the road and tipping my hat to the first lady that came along in the days when getting sunburnt was unheard of and you would see women in long crinoline dresses and men in striped swimsuits. I'd love to have lived back in those days, when manners and values were the first thing in people's minds, you know, when manners were really built in with the plumbing.

'While I've been living in Prestatyn something that was dear to my heart and something that meant a lot to me happened, in 1985. Not only do I collect old postcards, I collect old advertising as well, and while looking in a dusty corner of a second-hand shop in Rhyl one day I came across this box and I was rooting through it and I came across a bonnet and apron with the word Ovaltine stitched in orange on it. And I asked the man where it had come from and he couldn't tell me, so I asked him how much he wanted for it and he told me and I couldn't get my hands in my pocket quick enough. You can still see the scorch-marks, look! Anyway, I came back with the bonnet and apron and I researched into the background and I found they originally belonged to the Ovaltine Dairymaid, the woman that's on the tins. The Ovaltine Dairymaid promoted Ovaltine... and anyway I researched a bit deeper into it and I found out that the original Ovaltine woman – her name was Bertha Gray – was still alive and living in a home in Prestatyn and I just couldn't believe it. So I went to see her and had a long chat with her and she told me all about how she promoted Ovaltine in the twenties. I asked her about that bonnet and apron, about how I'd found it in a second-hand shop and she said, "Oh, I was living in Rhyl and I got rid of a lot of things". And I asked her – eighty-five, I think she was – I asked to wear it, and she said, "No, you'd laugh at me", you know. So anyway, she wore the bonnet and apron and the people in the home got a catering can of Ovaltine from the kitchens and some photographs were taken and meeting her and talking about the old days, that's nostalgia. And that to me is what the past's all about, is nostalgia and she was a living legend really, you know. Sadly, she died in 1985, but I've got these photographs and I'm happy to say that she was living on my doorstep here. One thing she told me, by the way, that made me laugh was that she hated Ovaltine. She preferred Horlicks; it got her off to sleep quicker!

'I think if you research and dig into the past, there's an amazing amount of information you can dig out. Not only in

Prestatyn but in the whole of Wales. It's very, very important that we record this information. People always love reading about the past, and the past will always be there, won't it? I'm sure there are a lot more stories I can dig up. That's how I can explain Wales. It's the biggest treasure-hunt island of all time. We're here to discover it, I think, and that's how I find Wales. There's a story down every street and road and lane, not forgetting the most important lane of all, Memory Lane.'

Frances M. Welsh, Llandudno, Gwynedd

Frances Welsh is seventy-two. She was born and educated in Llandudno, her father's family originally from Pwllheli and her mother's from Wolverhampton. Apart from her years in the Wrens, she has lived there all her life, latterly on the West Shore. Her two children now live in the south of England.

I've noticed there are more people coming shopping in Llandudno now and I've overheard their conversations, saying it's one of the finest places for shopping. The big stores and everything are on the outskirts, but a lot of the little shops are now closing down and we seem to be getting a lot of these – not that I'm against it – these sort of bazaar-type shops in the main town itself. But I don't think it has changed so much . . . We have no stalls or anything like that on the beach, they don't allow those. The donkeys are still there. In fact, one of the original donkey men died last week and he was 93 and he had a burial with the old hansom cabs which his father used to give rides along the beach with.

'My father was born on the Great Orme in 1895 and worked in the St George's Hotel from the age of eleven. It was one of the first hotels in Llandudno. My Grandmother worked in the laundries in the hotels. This is how most people in Llandudno worked in those days; there wasn't much else. The men ran the boat trips out along the bay and in the winter they painted them. My father went to the National School, so did I and my children, it's now the Library. Then there was the old school, Grammar School, which I was educated in and so were my children: John Bright. It's now a comprehensive, and has changed so much. . . There was a time if you went for an interview at university and you said you had gone to John Bright Grammar School, you were in, but I don't think that's the case now. When I was at school, you *had* to learn Welsh, we had to sit a scholarship paper in Welsh. When I went to John Bright, having passed the scholarship, unless you spoke Welsh at home you had to take French. You were not *allowed* to take Welsh. I think people should be given the option of learning another language, like French rather than Welsh. Now, I know enough Welsh to understand what people are saying, but if I try to say anything I go to French because that was the last language I learned.

'Personally I've never found it any advantage to speak Welsh. I went away to work, I went in to a bank at seventeen, and in those days women were not allowed to work in banks in their locality – they had to go a long way away – so I went to the Midlands, then I came back eventually to Colwyn Bay because women were then being allowed in, then I went to Penmaenmawr. But for me personally, the little bit of Welsh I learned – I mean I can read Welsh, I can understand a certain amount – I wouldn't say that it's ever stopped me from doing . . . in fact, I've never come across it outside Wales. Both my children had to learn Welsh, to a different standard from me because they went through grammar school – my son is a linguist – and they can both speak Welsh, for what they want.

'Welsh wasn't emphasised at all when I was growing up. I think it's only recent years that they've gone to town on it. Thinking back then, my brother went into the RAF at sixteen in 1936 or 1937. He had to sit an entrance exam because he went as an apprentice, and the Headmaster of John Bright *then* didn't want to know. In fact my brother had to remind him of the date he was to set him the paper. And it wasn't until afterwards, thinking back, that I found that this Welsh Nationalism was running through the school even then, and they would have influenced you if they could. Because he was against him sitting to go in the RAF, you see. It was at the time when I was at school that a minister from Llandudno and two other men blew up a bombing school in Llŷn, and that was the time that my brother was sitting the exam. As a child I wasn't aware of it, they didn't *dwell* on the Welsh when I was at school at all, it was part of it and you just took it. I don't know that my children have been influenced by it at all. I can't see that it's made any difference.'

Aled Williams, Llanfairfechan, Gwynedd*

Aled Williams is slightly-built, with a mop of dark hair and a pencil-line moustache which makes him look a good ten years younger than his thirty-five. He moved to Llanfairfechan from Bethesda twenty-two years ago when his family 'completely out of the blue` inherited eight acres and a house from an uncle. At seventeen he left home 'to find my own way in the world' and ended up in a series of menial jobs – van boy for a bakery, general labourer and for five years a storeman at Hotpoint in Llandudno. He now works as a nursing assistant at the Bryn y Neuadd hospital in the village, caring for people with learning difficulties.

'The best years in my life were 1976 to 1978. I got myself a guitar and me and some mates started a garage band. I think I was really lucky to be growing up at a time when the music was perfect – rock. Thin Lizzie, Supertramp, the whole thing. It was an age of innocence, really. And when I wasn't playing music I was out listening to it. Every Friday night it was bath and out – the Goat in Pen[maenmawr], the Winter Gardens, Llandudno and Dixieland, Rhyl. We'd just drink, bop and generally have a brilliant time. Saturday afternoons was the Llanfair Arms. The place was always heaving: music, cards, darts, the lot. I'd got my own place by then. A house in Llan that cost me eight grand. I did all the wiring, plastering and plumbing myself, learned on the job sort of thing. I still live there; fifty quid a month mortgage – can't be bad.

'I've been at Bryn y Neuadd for six years now. I started out just helping a mate who worked there and drifted into it. I love it. Every minute of it. It's the longest I've ever stayed in one job and it's the one I've had to think most in. It's made me more mature, definitely. I went there the first day, like, wanting to do a lot for them, but after six years in the place your expectations are less.

'I suppose it'll close before long. You know, with care in the community. I guess it's got about between four and six years left. I think that care in the community is a great idea if it's done properly. Say, two or three living together in the same house.

'If it closes, it closes. I could probably find something similar, but I'm not actually a qualified nurse. It'd take me three years to do that and I can't be bothered. What the hell? The bike's paid for and I could live happily enough on the dole. And I'd never consider moving for work. Yes, I suppose I'm optimistic about the future, because I don't expect that much. Don't be too hasty. Live from one day to the next, that's me.

'The best day in my life, the turning point, was passing my bike test at the second go four years ago. I've got a GSXR 750W. And my favourite hobby is riding it bloody fast. It frees you up, makes you independent. You get to know other bikers, just people in general. And the worst day, the biggest disappointment in my life, was last November when I wrecked it on a patch of black ice in Rhyl.'

How well do you know Wales?

'Put it this way. I've been through the Bermuda Triangle five times but I've never been to Cardiff.'

Avril Williams, Bangor, Gwynedd*

Avril Williams works as a cleaner in the Welsh hall of residence at University College, Bangor. She is forty-five and has dark hair and an almost Latin complexion. We spoke over a breaktime cup of tea in a noisy staffroom.

'There's not much to say. I've been working in the hall for ten years. I trained as a hairdresser after leaving school in the sixties and worked in Bangor's West End and at the Wellfield [shopping precinct]. I got married in 1969 and we've got two children, a son in the Royal Welsh Guards and a daughter working at Kwiks in Caernarfon. I've lived in Bangor all my life, well, Tregarth to start with. Dad's from Llandegfan and mam's from Tregarth. We moved to Bangor when I was three. Mam had her own hairdressing business and dad was a plumber. He'd worked on the railways for about ten years and then Beeching came in and there were redundancies, so he got out before the redundancies started and he worked for the Council and a bit of work for himself.

'I left work when I got married and had children. My husband's local, from Maesgeirchen. He's a joiner. '

And work now?

'It's changed since the hall changed from girls only to mixed. We find all sorts of things in the lads' rooms. I'd better not say what! It would be X-rated!

'I've never really wanted to live anywhere else. Mam and Dad thought about going to Australia when there was the boom at the end of the fifties, beginning of the sixties. And if they had moved, I could have been an Aussie, couldn't I?! The only relative I've got outside Wales is a cousin in Manchester, and he lived in Spain for six years. If I won the pools I'd still live here. I don't know the rest of Wales. I've never been to Cardiff. I've never been to Ireland . . . I've seen Scotland on television. From what I've seen of it, it's just like Wales: mountains and such like.

The accent's different of course. I haven't had a proper holiday in six years. Spain was the last one.'

So what does Wales mean to you?

'More now, I think. Since I've got older. We always spoke Welsh at home, but I went through a phase when I was younger. You know? If I'd got friends who spoke English I didn't like Mam speaking Welsh to me in front of them in town and suchlike. I thought it was old-fashioned. But now I speak it a lot more.'

Has working in a Welsh-medium hall had any effect?

'A bit. But even when this hall was all English all the staff were Welsh, and we always speak Welsh with one another – and keep the language going. But at home, it's English. My mother-in-law's from Manchester, so . . . My children didn't speak much Welsh when they were younger, but my son has changed a lot and he's become more proud of the language. He's in Ireland and he's been there two years, on what they call a long tour of duty. So I'm looking forward to him coming out. He's going to Tern Hill, near Shrewsbury.'

Once the tape recorder is turned off, she grimaces in mock agony and ambarrassment. The cleaner next to her sups her tea stoically. 'Turn that thing on for me, cariad,*' she says, 'and I'll tell you what we find in the boys' rooms.'*

David Williams, Machynlleth, Powys*

On an otherwise quiet Sunday afternoon in Machynlleth it is impossible to ignore the buzz of activity around Y Tabernacl, the town's cultural centre, opened some ten years ago. A simple shop front leads through to a well-lit exhibition area and on again to a bar where nearly a hundred people are enjoying a Tuscan Lunch, one of the events arranged by the centre to launch the Machynlleth Festival. Collecting tickets at the door is a man with a neat moustache and glasses who appears to know everyone. Originally from Caernarfon, he moved to the area with his work and stayed when he became a safety officer with the old Merioneth County Council. He retired eighteen months ago.

'I've got time on my hands and so I contribute some of that time to *Y Tabernacl*. Every now and then they have exhibitions like you see here today and they want someone to be here just to keep an eye on things and I contribute by giving them an afternoon or whatever here and there.

'*Y Tabernacl* was the idea of the Owen Owens family originally. You know, Owen Owens, Liverpool? The big store in Liverpool? Their home's up in Garth Winion, near Machynlleth here. And the family more or less felt, well we'll give a bit of culture to the town. And they started, of course, by buying the old chapel, *Y Tabernacl* – that's where the name came from – when it came empty. And, you know, it's nice to see a chapel turned to a purpose of this sort rather than become a garage or a warehouse or that sort of thing. And that's the root of it and now they've developed it, they've added to the building, bought the bit where we are now – this was an old shop – and then during the last twelve months they've put in an extension at the back of the shop which is attached to the chapel to make one unit. Now there's even a language laboratory at the back, up the stairs. In the chapel now there's four translation booths so you can have four meetings there at the same time. You can show films, hold concerts here and, you know, it's a cultural centre of that sort.'

What events are held here?

'Exhibitions are the basis of the place at the moment, but, you know, there were pensioners here a year or two ago – the Welsh Pensioners' Parliament or something? And the sort of thing you see here today.'

Do local people use the Centre directly?

'Yes, they do. Even the local choirs practise here, you see. And there are local concerts by the choirs and so on. And the place is appreciated. They've just created Friends of *Y Tabernacl*. The idea was that money was scarce and there were fears that the place was going to close. So what they did was to create this and everybody contributed £5, £10 or whatever it was and the support locally, well it's excellent. A large number of the town's people have contributed towards this because they realise I think that it's . . . well, that it's something unique for somewhere that's in essence a village. And people come in – especially visitors, especially English people – and they say, "This is a miracle". You know? That things of this standard are available in such a small place. Remote in a way. But I believe that the people of the town appreciate it, too, that they've got something special.'

Events in English and Welsh?

'Yes indeed. Yes, strongly bilingual. I think that's a healthy policy – correct bilingualism. I don't like to see a bias either way. There is certainly a strong, lively bilingual policy.

'Machynlleth is a place that developed particularly with the railways. When the railway came through from Newtown it changed the place completely. Before then it was the agricultural centre for the Dyfi Valley area, for sheep and what have you, with very little contact with the outside world. And then the railway came, you see and we lost all the old activities, the woollen mill, shoeing horses – they all went. And this place grew, like Swindon if you like: a railway town. A large proportion of the men in the town worked on the railway.

Someone was telling me just recently they remember three hundred and fifty going in through the station gates in the mornings, to *work*. Spreading out into the signal boxes and everywhere, and carrying stuff from the station to the houses – you know how they did in the old days? Door-to-door service. So it grew up like that. The GPO brought a big depot here, the engineering works in particular, they were very important here. Then the Forestry Commission came. Like most other towns in mid or rural Wales all of these industries are now decayed. The railway particularly has shed most of its workers, they've even gone on to radio signalling now, so the signal boxes are unmanned even. British Telecom is more or less on the brink of closing its depot in the town, because they have a policy of centralising. And the Forestry Commission is very much let out to contract labour, self-employed labour, which means that the town really is decayed. There are some new businesses opening; estate agents, as everywhere else, seem to dominate the high street. Yes, we have exotic newcomers, like Indian Restaurants – just opened this last week – but the old traditional style of the town is disappearing fast. For example, the triangle based on the clock, which is the centre of the business part of the town, is suffering from the coming in of a supermarket, Lo-Cost, which is three quarters of the way up the main street and, being a store that sells everything, it hits the newsagents, it hits the butchers, the florists, the greengrocers, you know all the small traditional shops are being hit by the superstore.

'Probably, in a direct sense, Y *Tabernacl* has very little impact on keeping the centre of a place like Machynlleth alive. But I would imagine, peripherally, it does have in the sense that it gives the town's people a sense of identity. This decentralisation from the town centre to the suburbs is in a sense, culturally at least, counteracted by the presence of this establishment, which is a *cultural* centre. And of course culture is so subjective that it attracts everyone, all classes, all social strata, everybody is in on it. The scope is quite wide. It tends to edge upwards rather than downwards, if you follow what I mean. I doubt if we'll ever have a stripper here or a fire-eater, but otherwise it's quite elastic in its range of presentations.'

David Williams, Builth Wells, Powys

When a stranger in a hotel bar, unprompted, asks you what defines a Welshman, the temptation to interview is irresistible. David Williams is fifty-three and works as a glass engraver and sculptor, travelling to Romania in his own time to paint murals for orphanages.

'If you look at this area, Builth in particular, which is in the centre of Wales, historically nobody came into these areas, they all moved away. If anybody wanted to make it they moved out. There's just one or two of the old families stayed here. It was a farming community. If you wanted to go down the mines you went down south, down to the melting pots. So if you classed anybody from this area as an animal, he'd be a thoroughbred. If you take Anglesey and all the coastal areas you've got Vikings, Danes, Scots and Irish – a terrific mixture of blood. Now, is it the blood that makes a person or what he speaks makes a person? That's the main point really. It isn't what a man speaks, it's what's in his heart that really counts. And I mean, my family has lived here for, what, three hundred-odd years, I suppose, in Builth. My mother's family came from Rhaeadr. The graves are there for the old family, the Webbs, from 1790, so they are Welsh people. Just let somebody from Anglesey come down here and say, "Oh, you don't speak Welsh, you're not a Welshman" – I'm born in the heart of Wales, that is only now being opened up to people moving in.'

How strong a sense of Welshness do people in this area have?

'Oh, the old families, very much so. We don't speak Welsh because most of our trading has been done with Herefordshire and we moved to that area as opposed to down on the coastal areas. We always looked to Hereford as the main town. It still is for the main shopping area today. We are border counties. Now, you take a dialect like Radnorshire. They talk about the Welsh language, it's a great shame that the old Radnorshire dialect is dying out because I heard on the radio a programme of Shakespeare where they said Shakespeare isn't spoken in this

BBC English; it's spoken in what they call *Old* English. And when I heard this programme and the way they were speaking I thought, that's *Radnorshire* and I could understand it when it was spoken like that when it's difficult to understand when it's spoken in BBC English. Yes, this part of Wales is very Welsh and very proud of its roots. It is unfortunate that we don't speak Welsh. I think that my grandparents did because the old Bible is Welsh, but my parents never spoke it and Welsh wasn't taught in the schools either. French was the language to learn in the schools.

'I'm very proud of being Welsh. I go to Romania a couple of times a year and I have to explain to them that I'm not English. I always wave the flag of Wales, and yet it is very annoying when somebody comes down, particularly from north Wales, and says, "You're not Welsh" and my ancestors were born and bred here. Theirs have come from Liverpool – or Norway or somewhere like that on a longboat.'

Why has Welshness in this part of Wales never found political expression?

'Because – and this is very much my personal opinion – Plaid lean very much to the left and they are fanatical about Welsh speaking. If you speak Welsh you are a Welshman. If I was black and spoke Welsh I would be a Welshman. *My* heritage doesn't count. If I was an Eskimo, let's say, and I came here and I learned to speak Welsh, would I be a Welshman or an Eskimo? I think Welsh *is* very important, but you mustn't ram it down people's throats. There was a time when the cheque book went bilingual through a small minority insisting. Well, I went to the bank and I said, "There's words on here I don't understand; I want an English one." Because I would dearly love to speak Welsh, but which do I speak, north Wales or south Wales? When they sort it out themselves . . . And they say you should have all this written in Welsh, all these signs and what have you. I saw an incident at the [Royal Welsh] Showground, where somebody said about one of my signs, "This should be bilingual," and I said, well write it out for me, tell me what it should say. And then it was, "Well, er, I can't actually write . . . I don't know the word to use for this and that . . ." So until they sort that out . . .

'We are very tribal and very territorial . . . as a nation. We've got north Wales, south Wales; there's rivalry. Then you take the county of Powys; you've got Breconshire, Radnorshire, Montgomeryshire. I'm a Breconshire boy; I'm nothing to do with Radnorshire although I will, in certain circumstances . . . but Montgomeryshire I don't want to know. I don't want somebody up in Llanfyllin making decisions for me. And you can also break it down to village, to town. Builth and Llandrindod: there's always been rivalry. As a nation we are very tribal. We are Welshmen when we're outside. When we're here we're either north Wales or south Wales, or you're a Breconshire boy or you're a Builth boy or a Llandrindod boy. We do have an identity, but we start arguing about who we are.'

If Wales is so tribal, is there any common ground?

'There's three things a Welshman has that an Englishman can never have: there's *hwyl, hiraeth* and the ability to *cwtsh.*'

Meira Williams, Pentrefoelas, Clwyd*

Ann Owen at the Information Centre says that Meira Williams is 'a good talker' and telephones ahead. Meira agrees, and is waiting outside her house when I arrive, a neat semi that was once a council house. She is forty-two, with bright eyes and an infectious smile. We go through to the dining kitchen and she clears a space at the table. When a neighbour arrives and settles down to watch proceedings Meira has second thoughts and tries to persuade me, the neighbour and herself that a native of the village would make a better interviewee. We both disagree.

'I was born in a little village outside Llansannan called Tan y Fron – a tiny, tiny village, much smaller than Pentrefoelas. Dad was born on a farm and was one of nine children and he was the youngest, and mam was an only child. I was brought up on a smallholding, a little place. There was a chapel in the village and a school. We had to walk a mile to school and back.

'I came to Pentrefoelas when I got married. Dwyfor works for the County Council, driving a lorry. I work in an old people's home in Pandy Tudur at the moment. It holds thirty-one, but at the moment I think we've got four empty beds. I go there in the evenings to give them their supper and put them to bed. I arrive there at five and finish at ten. Most of the people come from around Llangernyw. It's a very Welsh old people's home, you know. There's more Welsh than English there. And I've got two girls, one eighteen and the other fifteen. Perhaps where work's concerned we lose out. You have to travel everywhere, don't you? Especially the two girls, when they're looking for work. They have to travel out of Pentrefoelas, don't they? Siân's got work in the shop, helping out in the shop, but Olwen, she's just done her A Levels and at the moment Olwen's having to travel to Rhuthun. She's got work with Dodds the estate agents in Rhuthun, full-time. So she's having to go all the way to Rhuthun. But otherwise, it's nice and quiet here. I wouldn't like to live in the middle of a town at all. It's nice and quiet and you know everybody around you and suchlike, not like you would in a town. I've lived here . . . twenty years. Yes, must be twenty years.'

Has the village changed much in that time?

'Well. yes, to tell you the truth. Ever since Berwyn Evans has been busy here. He's altered it a lot, you know. *Menter Hiraethog* started it all off. They've re-done the mill, and there's Berwyn's office at the bottom of the village. There's places for twenty at the factory and there's lots of little workshops at the back . . . what do you call them? . . . little huts. There's a man making candles there, there's a woodworker, there's people doing soft furnishings – curtains and such. And I think that all the units – that's the word – are full now.'

Local people?

'No. The only local one is Menna. There's a local girl, a farmer's wife, Menna Hafod y Dre, she's taken the old butcher's shop over. Doing embroidery designs and such. I think she's very busy.'

Has Pentrefoelas remained Welsh?

'Oh, yes. Yes. We're very lucky. It's mostly Welsh round here. Yes, we're very lucky.'

If you could change one thing to improve life in Pentrefoelas, what would it be?

'More things for young people to do, I think. They've got the school and Menna – the embroidery lady – she's got the young farmers' club. But apart from that, there's not much. It's alright in the winter, but the summer's quiet for them.'

When the interview is over Meira asks what precisely I'm going to do with it. When I explain she tells me that her father is mentioned in I Bought a Mountain. *'Just a little piece like that,' she says, holding finger and thumb an inch apart. 'It said he was good with a gun when he was a farmhand.'*

W. Penri Williams, Llanbrynmair, Powys*

The two ladies in the park at Llanbrynmair agree that 'Peni' Williams would be a good speaker and they lead me to his bungalow. He is in the garden of a next door neighbour, discussing the best place to plant certain vegetables. When I explain my intention he invites me inside.

'I went out to work on the farms when I was fourteen years old. It was a poor time then, you see. This was 1927 and I remember going out to work on a not very big farm and they were old people – getting on a bit – and it didn't suit a young lad like me very well, did it? And the old woman said to me at the end of the year – we were employed for a year at that time, you see, thirteen pounds, *tair punt ar ddeg*, you lived in – and in a year's time she said to me, "We don't want you again," she said. "*Rwyt ti'n rhy ddrygiog*, you're too mischievous." That's what she said. And she was right, you know! Well, I went off, didn't I? I went to work on another farm then. This was quite a sizeable farm and there were lads like me there because this was a young couple. And I went there and it was fine there, living in with them and I was there for four years. And, "*Duw*," the boss says to me one day, "you know what?" he says, "I'm sorry to tell you this," he says, "the wife's brother wants your place." "Well, fair enough, " I said. And I went away and that was that. But he said to me about half a year later, "You know what?" he said, "if I'd known how it would be I'd have kept you on."

'So I went to another big place then – Glanhanog – with the Breeses. There were four of us working there, five very often. Enough work to do, mark you, and a little bit more pay now. I was earning about . . . well, fourteen shillings a week. And that's where I was for years, nine years. It was a good place, plenty of proper food there and everything. But they wanted a day of work out of you, a good day's work every day. There were two brothers owned it and they had plenty of money, a car and everything. But I rather felt like a change now and I left there and I went down to Towyn, to Merioneth, to a place belonging to a man called Llywelyn Williams. Two of my brothers had been working there before me and down I went.

'I arrived in 1939, the year the War broke out. Well, in September 1939 he had notice about the farm, that it was being used for the war effort. They came and levelled it out; it's still levelled out today. It's there today. I went from there then and went to another farm. Down near . . . do you know where Cader Idris is? With the Tudors. It was a fair enough place, but they boss was away every day – "buying cattle". And he was a councillor, you know, and a JP and held every job under the sun.

'Well, in 1941 we got married. She was a maid on a farm nearby with Ifan Anwyl, Tŷ Mawr, Towyn. And a place came free and we took it and that was that. We brought up four children – three girls, one boy – and we took on another farm then and a house . . . and I worked for the council then *and* farmed two farms. *Diawl,* I was working night and day! There was no end to it! And two years ago I gave it up. Of course I've been retired sixteen years, I'm eighty-one. And I've never been in bed a day. No, never. Never lost a day at work, working for the council, too, for twenty years. I still keep sheep, one hundred and thirty head – two hundred with the lambs. I've sold all the cattle, done away with them, but I've still got three dogs and a nephew of mine goes there when he's not working in Newtown. He's there today or I'd have been up there now.

'I've seen some hard times, but it's improved now, as things *do* improve. I've never bothered with pubs and suchlike, never had much trouble with that job, thank goodness. And that's how my life's been. But, all things considered, I've been *lwcus ddychrynllyd*, dreadfully lucky with my health. I'm not complaining. I really can't complain. And like they say, *heb iechyd, baich yw bywyd* – "without good health life's a burden." I know some in Llanbrynmair here now; they're only about sixty-five and they're not good at all. They'll never work again like they used to. Our life's very uncertain, isn't it? Very uncertain. What'll happen to me from now on I don't know. Nobody knows, do they? That's my days for you. There.'

Harry Woosnam, Llanbister, Powys

When I met Mr Harry Woosnam he was standing chatting to the men repairing the retaining wall around Llanbister War Memorial, showing more than a casual interest in the proceedings. He invited me into his bungalow where photographs of five generations of his and his wife's families cover the walls. A french window looks west across to Abbeycwmhir.

I've lived round here – all but three years – all of my life and I'm seventy-four now next birthday. There's Tinboeth Castle up there, though you can't see it now, too misty, and I've been in sight of that all but three years. I came with my mam and dad when I was a little baby of six months old, they were at Llaithddu. I did farm work around this area for Watsons of Llananno, five years, first of all for my uncle up at Llaithddu for eighteen months, and I went out at fourteen. I worked for Williamsons for fourteen years, all sorts of work, sheep, cattle, hedging and so on. Then I went to the council, Radnorshire County Council first, then Powys. I went in 1957, I had twenty-eight years. Roadworks – same as these boys out here – walling and bridgebuilding. Here's one down here that I built with the gang. There it is, see? There. We were five in the gang and we built stone walls, things like that. I went to Special Foreman and Bridge Foreman and then Supervisory Foreman and then I finished, I retired. There's still plenty to do, like. I keep the garden tidy and I help my son-in-law and daughter at The Pound; it's a little farm they've got, like. I lost my first wife at forty-five – I've got two children, a boy and a girl – and I married again. And Mary was married before. I knew her before, years ago . . . not at school with her, but we knew them, the family. And also we are great-grandparents, and there's the photos there, if you want to see them. That's the great-grandchildren and that's my grandson. He passed for an accountant and now he's teaching with his wife now, two teachers. And that's Mary's three girls – grandchildren and that's a niece of hers. And over there, that's *all* the family. Pull it down, pull it down. Take a proper look . . . that's my grandsons. This one is farming in Pembroke and that's the one in Cardiff and he's in Cardiff as well. All the boys are away now. I think I'll start looking for photos now, being I'm started on that. Can that machine still hear what I'm saying . . . ?'

At that point the photo albums are brought out, snapshots and cuttings taken from drawers, the family archive opened.

'See that man and woman there? That's when I was working at Bryndu, Llananno, for that man. And he was ninety last October and he sent the photo of him and his wife, still living. And I do their lawns now. I've got more photos here now I've been getting out for another man today. You see what they were doing at the Monument? There it is before it was changed. That's what they're walling now. And I cut the monument, keep the grass clean. It's all built in here now. Now then . . .'

Mr Woosnam shows me a newspaper photograph of the opening of a bridge. A row of men stand in front of a tape, smiling, eyes closed against the sunlight.

'I built that bridge, it's the last bridge of Radnorshire County Council, at Penybont, around 1972 or 1973, then we went on to Powys County Council. That's all the workman and the County Surveyor and Councillors . . . Now, what else have I got here? I'm taking your time now, am I? And I've had this one enlarged, see. There you are . . . what else have I got here? Now here's the men that won the war. I'm in there somewhere. Where do you think I am? There's me and that's my brother-in-law. Home Guard, based in Llanbister.'

Did anything ever happen to keep you busy?

'No not really . . . well we were fighting them off, you know? If we was here they didn't come near we, like.'

Harry Woosnam fishes out a photograph of a formally posed group, mother, father and child. The child, no more than one year old, is standing, supported by his mother, wearing stout black boots and a large white collar over a dark knickerbocker suit. On the back, in fountain pen, are the words 'Mr and Mrs G. Woosnam and Harry.'

'Now then, that's me there, see? I wouldn't have been more than about twelve months or eighteen months, I think. The wife I've got now, she laughs at my shoes in this one . . . and there's another gang. Can you pick me out? And this one, I treasure it. And this is from the party in 1985 when I retired.'

Mr Woosnam hands me a letter thanking him for 'twenty-eight years of loyal and dedicated service' and a poem written by his colleagues . . .

> When you travel through Radnor you should keep a look out
> For a small yellow van you may see round about.
> It's parked in the roadway, on the verge of the lane.
> The public complaining 'It's Harry again!'
>
> There's no telling when you'll see Harry appear
> From the Cox Head to Dolau, from far and from near;
> His pipe will be smoking as he speeds on his way
> 'There's trouble at Dutlas,' you'll hear Harry say.
>
> But now we find Harry the foreman has gone,
> No more will he wander no more will he roam.
> No worry of shovels, of posts and fence wire -
> Harry's decided it's time to retire.
>
> It's the cold winds of winter as we measure their might,
> The road men with shovels turn out in the night.
> As the gritters speed northwards on the A483
> For the roads are kept open for you and for me.
>
> Should you go to Llanbister in the midst of all snow
> I'm told to Pound alehouse you always can go,
> For up on the road there with an army of men
> That convoy of snow ploughs are at it again.

They plough from the Gravel to the old City shop
For they're under instruction there never to stop.
These men are the backbone, the strength of the nation,
Ploughing from Crossways to Llangunllo Station.

We have a small depot at Graeantwyndir
And a small yellow van to which I've referred;
A division alone, set aside from the rest,
The surveyors call Harry, he's one of the best.

Then farewell to Harry as he leaves to retire
He helped out the boss when he was in the mire.
If the forthcoming winter leaves snow on the ground
Will we find Harry ploughing from Moelfre to Pound?

Then it's bed for a fortnight to recover his pose,
His wife helps herself as the need it arose.
He built fourteen bridges in foul weather and fair,
When we have all gone they'll still be standing there.

Jeff Young, Porthcawl, Mid Glamorgan

Jeff Young was born in a mining family in Blaengarw and is a former Welsh RU international. His first job was teaching in a public school in Harrogate, where he met and married his wife. He joined the Air Force in 1971 and after twenty years retired to take up the job of Technical Director of the Welsh Rugby Union in 1991. We spoke in the 'Dragon Wagon', the WRU's mobile promotion vehicle, on the Eisteddfod field in Neath.

'I started playing in the primary school in Blaengarw with a great man called Chick Jones who taught pottery and rugby and he was my first mentor in the game. I went from there to the Garw Grammar School and came into contact with another magnificent rugby man who still lives in Blaengarw called John Rees and interestingly enough I met both those people for the first time in twenty years about six months ago. Mr Chick Jones is now eighty-five and still has a most magnificent mind, not only for rugby but for the arts of Wales and so has Mr John Rees and both were in good heart and good health. I then was fortunate enough to play international rugby while I was at the Garw Grammar School and it was only because Mr John Rees drove me around to the trials. My parents didn't have a car and if Mr Rees hadn't done that then I wouldn't have gone to the trials and played for Wales as a secondary schoolboy. I was very fortunate in playing at under fifteen level and under eighteen level for the schools. I played hooker – the most intelligent position on the field (!) And from there I went to St Luke's College Exeter and played rugby there for the college, went to Harrogate, played my rugby at Harrogate, captained Yorkshire in the County Championships. I was noticed by the selectors during that time, came down for some trials – in those days we used to have trials for the Welsh national side – and I then got my first cap in 1968. Fortunately that was the year that the Lions were going to South Africa so I joined that trip as a Lion as well and then played up until 1973 when a neck injury forced me to retire – just wear and tear as a result of scrummaging in the game.

'My present job is based in the Welsh Rugby Union Headquarters in Cardiff and the responsibilities with that include the development of coaching, the promoting of the game which we think is the game of Wales, and to identify and develop the better players in Wales and then to provide direct support to our national squads – all seven of them, I might add! Because from the Wales side at the top end down to our schools Under 16 team we have international sides between those ages. It's a good structure. I have eight Development Officers located strategically round Wales and their roles are to identify and develop the coaches based in the Welsh Rugby Union districts, to identify and develop players, to visit schools and clubs, to provide advice, and to assist clubs and schools in the development of the game. So we have an organization, perhaps we don't have as many Development Officers as I would want, nevertheless we have a structure *nationally* based on Welsh rugby at district level that enables us to get into the real grass roots of the game, not only with the Development Officers, but the Development Officers have support from a mass of volunteers in each district who are prepared to give up their time and use their goodwill and their expertise at no cost. Without the grass roots, the schools and the clubs, rugby wouldn't exist. We can play county rugby, district rugby, international rugby, but it all has to start somewhere. It starts at the schools and the clubs in Wales and they are the roots of our game.'

There is a common perception that in recent years Welsh Rugby, at international level, has been in decline. Is this true of the grass roots?

'It depends what your indicators are and how you measure that. Certainly if you measure it by the top end of the game, by the performance of the Wales team, then certainly we haven't been as successful as we would have liked, and *certainly* not as successful as we've been in past years. So perhaps the word decline may be appropriate . . . I'd like to think that we've addressed that decline. I came into the job in 1991 and Wales had just come back from Australia and had been beaten pretty heavily and there were criticisms of the behaviour off the field. That was a completely new picture to me, because I'd been used to a Welsh international side that was both successful on the field and really were expected to be good ambassadors for Wales off the field. I am confident now that we have a national structure to identify and develop international players and potential international players for the future.

'The main cause for optimism is the changed attitude of our players at the top end, in terms of their commitment, their fitness, their attention to detail, in terms of their skill. They are very, very aware of the need for a good performance. Also the immense amount of goodwill, support and assistance that is readily available throughout Wales for the game. And the important thing is to respect that, and to respect those people and to pay due tribute to them. When I came into the job in 1991 there was an air of depression in the game generally, which was reflected by the poor results of the Welsh team at the top; but now if you look today, you know, mums, dads, grandmothers, babies and other children, they're coming in and looking at the Dragon Wagon and just being part of the game of rugby and I think that the game is such an essential fabric of the Welsh way of life that it's not only about playing the game on the field, it's about the friendship, the team-work, the goodwill that is generated by the game itself. I'm very optimistic about people's spirit towards the game in Wales.'

What inroads is the game making in the north?

'We have a Development Officer up there in Wrexham, Austin Thomas, and the numbers of schools who have taken up the game there in recent years has increased. We are fighting a major battle against soccer of course . . . and, I might add, with rugby league because the main rugby league area is not very far away And all of the clubs in north Wales have taken on the responsibility of developing the youngsters. We're delighted that we seem to have got a lot of good people on our side.'

'I've had some really magnificent times . . . a real highlight of my life playing for Wales as I'm sure any international player would tell you and I met some wonderful people both in the Welsh side and among the opposition. No matter how old I get, and even on my death bed, I shall always look back and think that my marriage, the birth of my children and playing for Wales were the three major achievements of my life.'